STOCK MARKET

101

FROM **BULL AND BEAR MARKETS**
TO **DIVIDENDS**, **SHARES**, AND
MARGINS — YOUR ESSENTIAL
GUIDE TO THE **STOCK MARKET**

MICHELE CAGAN, CPA

Adams Media
New York   London   Toronto   Sydney   New Delhi

Adams Media
An Imprint of Simon & Schuster, Inc.
57 Littlefield Street
Avon, Massachusetts 02322

For information about special discounts for bulk purchases, please contact Simon & Schuster Special Sales at 1-866-506-1949 or business@simonandschuster.com.

The Simon & Schuster Speakers Bureau can bring authors to your live event. For more information or to book an event contact the Simon & Schuster Speakers Bureau at 1-866-248-3049 or visit our website at www.simonspeakers.com.

Manufactured in the United States of America

10   9   8   7   6   5

Library of Congress Cataloging-in-Publication Data has been applied for.

ISBN 978-1-4405-9919-4
ISBN 978-1-4405-9919-0 (ebook)

Contains material adapted from the following title published by Adams Media, an Imprint of Simon & Schuster, Inc.: *The Everything® Investing Book, 3rd Edition* by Michele Cagan, CPA, copyright © 2009, 2005, 1999 by F+W Media, Inc., ISBN 978-1-59869-829-9.

CONTENTS

INTRODUCTION

From the outside, the stock market seems to be a chaotic stew of mysterious numbers and larger-than-life personalities, a place where billions of dollars trade hands every day. But look a little closer, and you'll see the personal tales of triumph and failure, murder and suicide, fortunes won and lost. Throughout the market's storied history you'll find investors who made billions of dollars and investors who lost everything.

The stock market has been home to corporate scandals spurred by tremendous greed, scams and schemes, and insider trading. But it is also the place where dreams can come true, where a small start-up can experience a meteoric rise toward blue chip fame.

Armed with the right knowledge, any investor can profit in the stock market, and learn how to protect himself from unscrupulous con artists and deceitful brokers.

THE STOCK MARKET

Where Fortunes Are Won and Lost Every Day

It's where fortunes are won and lost, where anyone has a chance to strike it rich or lose everything: The stock market fuels dreams of building great wealth, but can turn suddenly, crushing those hopes and decimating nest eggs.

From the opening bell at 9:30 A.M. Eastern Standard Time to the market's close at 4:00 P.M., the U.S. stock markets never stop moving. The action, though, is nearly silent, a stark contrast to the "Wild West" excitement that characterized the markets as recently as ten years ago. Today, the quiet hum of computer screens has replaced the cacophony of shouting traders and the flurry of paper littering the floor.

THE U.S. MARKET IS BORN

When the United States was in its infancy, the founding fathers worked tirelessly to create a nation like no other. In a brilliant move, President George Washington installed Alexander Hamilton as the first Secretary of the Treasury in 1789. Under his watch, the U.S. stock market was born. Hamilton founded the country's first stock exchange in Philadelphia in 1790, followed shortly after by the New York Stock Exchange in 1792, where the Bank of New York was the first corporate stock traded.

The markets that now make up what is commonly known as the U.S. stock market are the New York Stock Exchange (NYSE) and the National Association of Securities Dealers Automated Quotations (NASDAQ). Other cities like Boston, Chicago, Philadelphia, Denver,

San Francisco, and Los Angeles have exchanges, as do many major international cities like London and Tokyo.

A Real Wall

Wall Street came by its name honestly: In 1685, it was positioned behind a twelve-foot stockade wall designed to protect the local Dutch settlers from the dangers of Native American and British attacks.

Though the United States still lays claim to the largest stock market in the world, emerging markets around the globe are rapidly adding to the number of publicly traded companies. All around the world, more than 600,000 companies are publicly traded, with billions of shares changing hands every day. By understanding how the different stock markets work and compete for your investment dollars, you'll be better equipped to succeed in the investing world.

Competition, both domestic and global, continues to make stock transactions more transparent and more accessible to all investors.

Greed . . . Is Good

Hollywood loves to stoke stock market drama, often portraying investment bankers and stockbrokers as cutthroat manipulators. One of the most quoted is Gordon Gekko from the movie *Wall Street*, famous for his core belief: "Greed, for lack of a better term, is good. Greed is right. Greed works."

Back in the 1990s, it became clear that individual investors were becoming serious players in the world of Wall Street. With the advent of online investing and an aggressive play for smaller investors by the two leading stock markets in the United States, the NYSE and the NASDAQ, buying and selling investments has gotten easier and much less expensive.

When people talk about Wall Street or "The Market," they're generally referring to the secondary trading market, where the vast majority of investors buy and sell stock. But the primary market is where it all begins. The main difference between these two markets are the players involved: In the primary market, large investors are buying shares of stock directly from the issuing company; in the secondary market, investors buy and sell shares from each other.

PRIMARY MARKET

When a privately owned company wants to raise a lot of money, the kind of funding required to help the company grow to its full potential, its owners may turn to an investment banker. Unlike brokers who help facilitate trades on the secondary market, investment bankers guide companies down Wall Street, helping them turn privately owned businesses into publicly traded companies.

This primary market is where stocks are actually created and sold—which is called "floated"—to the public for the first time. The first sale of stock by a company to the public is an initial public offering, or IPO. And though technically these IPO shares are sold to the public, it's not to the general public; rather, these shares are mainly sold to large institutional investors that have the kind of capital the issuing company is trying to raise.

SECONDARY MARKET

Everyday trading takes place on the secondary market, what people think of as the stock market. These trades take place on the major stock exchanges all around the world, such as the NYSE, the NASDAQ, and the London Stock Exchange (LSE).

Here, in the secondary market, trades take place between investors, without the involvement of the issuing companies. For example, if you buy shares in Coca-Cola, you're purchasing those shares from another investor; the Coca-Cola Company itself is not directly involved in the transaction.

Ticker Trivia

When a company purchases its own shares on the secondary market, it's called a stock buyback.

WHY STOCKS MAKE SENSE

Though stocks are often perceived as risky investments, over time they've performed better than any other type of security, even better than gold. Over the course of more than 200 years (from 1802–2002), stocks have returned an average 6.6% annually, while bonds have returned 3.60%, and gold only 0.7%. What's more, this is true the whole world over, not just in the United States. For long-term real returns, you really can't beat the stock market.

In the short-term, stock returns can be volatile, but that's not unexpected. What most people don't realize, though, is that other securities, even those that are supposed to be safer, suffer that same fate. Bonds, for example, also see wide swings in returns when looked at for short periods.

The highest long-term returns make stocks very attractive to investors and financial planners alike, but they're not the only reason that owning stocks makes sense. With literally thousands of publicly traded companies trading in the United States alone, there's a huge variety of stocks to choose from, making it easy to have a diversified portfolio. With the wealth of easily available information at your fingertips, you can find technical, historical, and analytical data at a moment's notice, helping you keep track of your investments with very little effort.

Then there's the cash benefit: Stocks are among the easiest assets to liquidate, meaning when you need cash, you can get it fast. On top of that, many stock investments, referred to as income stocks, also pay out regular dividends, providing investors with a steady and reliable stream of cash. In fact, many dividend rates are higher than the interest rates on bonds.

That said, the stock market can have nerve-wracking swings (where prices move erratically, like a pinball), exciting run-ups (when prices climb ever higher), and devastating downfalls (where prices plummet). Short-term fluctuations are bound to happen, but sticking with stocks for the long haul is still the surest way to see the best returns.

POLITICS AND THE STOCK MARKET

In the midst of an election year, particularly one marked by pronounced uncertainty, the overall market tends to decline.

Once a new president is elected and takes over, the market tends to follow a fairly predictable pattern. Normally, the first year of a first term brings market volatility as the new administration settles in. The second year in office normally brings mild overall gains, followed by stronger returns in the third year; on average, but not always, stock prices tend to increase by about 17% during the third year of a first term. By the second term, returns begin to settle down, though still increase to an average above 10% a year. Then, volatility comes back as the election season gets underway, leading to more shallow returns. Since 1833, average returns in an election year hover near 6%, though occasionally they've dipped down to negative returns.

Ticker Trivia

Presidents Barack Obama and Bill Clinton both saw market values increase by more than 50% during their terms.

Presidential term stages aren't the only factors that influence the stock market. Who ends up in the Oval Office has a clear impact as well, most notably along party lines. For example, for more than 100 years, the stock market has done better with Democrats in the White House (according to www.nasdaq.com). Under Democratic leadership, the Dow Jones Industrial Average, a key measure of stock market health (more on that in The Dow chapter), has posted average returns of 82.7%, compared with much tamer average returns of just 44.8% with a Republican at the helm.

CORPORATE SCANDALS AND THE STOCK MARKET

Crooked CEOs and corporate fraud make for explosive headlines and gripping TV dramas. They also can have definite and lasting effects on stock prices and the stock market as a whole, especially following news footage of fat cat executives being hauled away in handcuffs.

What's more, the fallout from a corporate scandal can fill newscasts and websites for several years, keeping the company's dirty laundry in the public eye and their stock price on the decline, according to a Stanford University study. That study looked at the impact of thirty-eight damaging CEOs, all at the forefront of scandals (including thirteen cases of outright lying, eight cases of sexual impropriety, and six cases of questionable finances) that took place between 2000 and 2015. Though only about half of the executives eventually stepped down or were fired, all of their companies took stock price hits.

While some corporations are permanently damaged or destroyed by scandal, others rise above the fray and thrive. Whether the story comes from the inner workings of the corporation or from a negative external event, the type of scandal (they're not all caused by questionable CEO behavior) and the steps the company takes to fix the problem make all the difference.

- The tainted Tylenol scare of 1982 caused Johnson & Johnson (JNJ) stock to plummet 17% when several deaths were linked to their popular product. By facing the public scrutiny head-on, and dealing with the problem (which, as it turned out, was not caused by anything the company did), the corporation was able to quickly salvage its reputation and watch its stock price rebound in about four months.
- The *Exxon Valdez*, an oil tanker, crashed into the Bligh Reef on Alaska's Prince William Sound on March 28, 1989, spilling millions of gallons of oil. This environmental catastrophe was

blamed overwhelmingly on corporate negligence, and analysts expected ExxonMobil's (XOM) stock to tank. But it didn't. In fact, even after the corporation was slapped with the biggest fine in history—initially $5 billion in punitive damages—its share price barely dipped by about 4%, and rebounded very quickly. That relatively minor reaction came because the tragic spill happened before Twitter and Instagram, so people weren't constantly reminded of it. On top of that, the Supreme Court lowered their punitive damages to a measly $507.5 million, a boon to the corporation's bottom line.

- *E. coli* contamination forced the temporary closing of more than forty Chipotle Mexican Grill (CMG) restaurants in 2015, and that drove the company's stock price down. Through the first months of 2016, the stock price struggled, despite the company's commitment to safer food-handling practices. Sales dropped while food safety and legal costs increased, leaving the company with overall losses on the books. The company still has some hurdles to overcome, and investors remain wary, keeping the stock price nearly $200 per share lower than it was a year ago, a 27% drop (as of May 2016). Could the share price rebound to prescandal highs? That depends on how well and how fast the company restores consumer confidence.

- The Volkswagen emissions test scandal of 2015, which affected more than 10 million cars worldwide, led CEO Martin Winterkorn to step down as the corporation's stock price lost ground. With continuing recalls, an ever-increasing stack of lawsuits, promised payouts to VW owners, fines and penalties, and restrictions on VW diesel-model sales in the United States, it's no wonder the company is posting billion-dollar losses, or that its July 2016 stock price is down 48% from the same time in the previous year. Volkswagen AG (VOW3) shares, which trade on the German stock exchange, have been seeing volatile, up and down price movement for months. How they handle this scandal will determine which way the shares move next.

AFTER THE BELL

Just because the markets close each day doesn't mean trading activity has stopped. From after-hours trading (AHT) to news and announcements, investors around the world can get their financial fixes around the clock.

The Bell

Every trading morning at 9:30 A.M., a bell (like a school bell) is rung to signal the start of the action on the NYSE. Trading stops at precisely 4:00 P.M., at the closing bell.

After-hours trading means just what it sounds like: The purchase and sale of stocks outside normal trading hours on the exchanges. In the past, this activity was limited to large institutional investors and the super-rich, but now almost anyone can do it, thanks to the ease of electronic trading.

While this sounds like good news all around, AHT comes with some serious cautions. Because fewer people trade after hours than when the exchanges are open, the market is much less liquid, and wider bid-ask spreads (the difference between the highest price that a buyer is willing to pay for an asset and the lowest price for which a seller is willing to sell it) are common, and prices fluctuate more wildly. On the upside, traders can take advantage of breaking news without having to wait for the markets to open the next day.

FINRA

The Financial Industry Regulatory Authority, FINRA, protects U.S. investors by making sure that the entire American securities industry functions honestly and fairly. This is an enormous undertaking. The authority oversees all of the securities firms conducting business in the United States, and presides over all of the dealings that take place between traders, brokers, and investors.

A Very Big Job

As of 2016, FINRA oversees 3,941 securities firms and the more than 640,000 brokers who work for them.

FINRA is a relatively new player in the oversight game. It emerged in 2007 from the combination of two other ruling bodies: the NYSE regulatory committee and the National Association of Securities Dealers (NASD). Their mandate: "To detect and prevent wrongdoing in the U.S. markets."

As of 2016, FINRA manages up to 75 billion transactions every single day, and as a result paints a clear picture of the U.S. financial markets. With its comprehensive oversight, the agency doesn't miss a thing. In fact, thanks to their dedicated vigilance during 2015, FINRA:

- Initiated 1,512 disciplinary actions against investment firms and brokers
- Imposed $95.1 million in fines
- Sent more than 800 insider trading and fraud cases up to the SEC (the U.S. Securities and Exchange Commission)
- Returned $96.6 million of compensation to defrauded investors

While it may seem like FINRA and the SEC do the same thing, they don't. The SEC strives to ensure fairness for individual investors; FINRA oversees brokerage firms and stockbrokers, regulating the industry. Each agency works from a different angle to keep the markets honest. At the end of the day, though, the SEC also oversees FINRA.

The Scam Meter

Not sure if an investment is too good to be true? Test it out on FINRA's Scam Meter (http://apps.finra.org/meters/1/scammeter.aspx), an online tool that helps investors avoid fraudulent investments. By answering just four questions, you'll learn whether the prospect is on the up-and-up or a fraudulent scheme.

NYSE

The Racing Heart of Wall Street

More than 200 years ago, a group of twenty-four Wall Street merchants signed a document called the Buttonwood Agreement. The agreement laid out all the rules for buying and selling shares of public stock, including the price for a trading seat. Their rules, which transformed over time, are the framework for today's rules of trading and the foundation of the New York Stock Exchange (NYSE).

The NYSE, also known to insiders as the Big Board, is home to many prominent industry players like Wal-Mart Stores, Coca-Cola, and McDonald's. The Big Board is not a place for small companies. Among other requirements for inclusion on the NYSE, a company must have at least 1.1 million publicly traded shares of stock outstanding, with a market value of at least $100 million. It must show pretax income of at least $10 million over the three most recent fiscal years, and have had earnings of at least $2 million in the two most recent years.

Until around ten years ago, traders and brokers had to vie for coveted "seats" on the NYSE, but all that changed when it transformed into a publicly traded corporation. Now, those seats are actually equity memberships, though many still refer to them as seats. What hasn't changed: The same strict regulations govern which professionals may obtain one-year licenses to trade on the exchange, and regulators keep close tabs on their compliance and ethical behavior.

With more than $19 trillion in total market capitalization listed (as of April 2016), the NYSE is the largest stock exchange in the world by market capitalization, or market cap, which is the market value of a company in terms of its outstanding shares. The NYSE holds more than a quarter of the total worldwide equities market. Every day on the NYSE, more than 450 billion shares are available for trading.

THE OPEN OUTCRY SYSTEM QUIETS

The long-standing tradition of the open outcry trading system is the one portrayed by movies and TV shows, where we see swarms of traders wildly waving their arms and shouting at the tops of their lungs. That realistic portrayal of the NYSE auction market system (before computers took over), where sellers announce asking prices and buyers put forth bids, shows how the market works: The highest bid gets matched with the lowest ask, and the auction trade is completed. Understanding the ins and outs of the trading floor involves knowing what each player does, particularly customers, brokers, floor traders, and specialists.

A customer contacts a broker with a trade request. The broker connects with the floor trader. A floor trader follows the wishes of the broker and looks for the best bid or ask offer from the specialists. A specialist's job is to make sure the trading traffic flows smoothly by making it easy to trade a particular stock, and most specialists handle somewhere between five and ten stocks on any given day. A specialist is responsible for posting bid and ask prices (or quotes), maintaining an inventory of the stocks (to facilitate trading), and actually executing the trades. Specialists act like matchmakers for bidders and askers, connecting as many as possible. If necessary, they will even buy for and sell from their own supply of shares.

Today, instead of face-to-face contact, lively and loud haggling, and paper buy and sell pads, trades on the NYSE are all done electronically. Even so, the NYSE system follows a familiar pattern that remains ingrained in market culture. In today's market:

1. A customer contacts a broker, whether by phone or Internet, and tells the broker what stock he wants to buy or sell.
2. The broker contacts the floor trader with the order.
3. The floor trader brings that request to a specialist in that specific stock.
4. The trade gets written up and executed.

Despite frantic market activity, the trading floor itself is a calm, quiet place, its character forever changed by technology. The shouts of traders have been replaced by the quiet buzz of computers, and the floor seems more like the quiet room in a library than a melee.

EARLY DAYS: THE WHITNEY SCANDAL

Though the exchange is highly respected, it's seen scandal. Perhaps none have been as central as when NYSE president Richard Whitney was charged with embezzlement and sentenced to five to ten years in Sing Sing prison.

From 1930 to 1935, Whitney represented and managed the NYSE. Whitney, a hapless gambler, threw his money after everything from blue chips to penny stocks, incurring losses more often than not. In 1931, for example, his debt reached $2 million. Whitney borrowed from just about everyone he knew to offset those losses, then used the borrowed money to buy even more stock, even as the market collapsed around him.

When he could no longer count on friendly loans, Whitney turned to embezzlement, stealing from customers, the New York Yacht Club (of which he was the treasurer), and even close to $1 million from the NYSE's own Gratuity Fund.

Whitney's crimes were exposed after his term as NYSE president, when an audit uncovered his thieving ways. But something good came out of this stock market scandal: The SEC, then a brand-new government agency, set regulations to protect investors against crimes like his.

HISTORY OF THE NYSE

The NYSE, with the distinction of being the oldest stock exchange in the United States, is housed in a 36,000-square-foot facility in New York City's financial district.

Affected by world events, the exchange has seen its share of heart-stopping ups and downs, some of the biggest occurring in just the last thirty years:

- On October 19, 1987, the Dow plummeted 22.61%, the largest one-day percentage drop in history.
- On October 27, 1997, the Dow took a 554-point nosedive, triggering for the first time the NYSE "circuit breaker" rule, created to halt all trading activity when it looks like the market might be headed for a crash.
- On March 16, 2000, the NYSE saw the Dow climb 499 points in a single day, the largest one-day gain in history.

- After the September 11, 2001, terrorist attacks, the NYSE closed for four days, followed by a Dow drop of 685 points, the largest one-day decline in points.

In 2007, the NYSE combined with the European stock exchange Euronext, to form NYSE Euronext, a global milestone for the trading community. This market broke a new record, trading more than 5 billion shares in a single day, on August 15, 2007, when trading volume hit an unprecedented 5,799,792,281 shares.

Not content to rest on its laurels, NYSE Euronext acquired the American Stock Exchange (AMEX) in 2008, and fully integrated trading began in early 2009. That combined exchange offered expanded trading capabilities, including stock options, exchange-traded funds, and other specialized securities.

Then, in 2013, everything changed. After more than 200 years of ruling the financial markets, the NYSE was bought by Intercontinental Exchange (ICE). Though it still operates as it did before the takeover, the NYSE is now just a holding in another company's portfolio.

NASDAQ

The Exchange That Launched 1,000 Tech Companies

It was the first of its kind, operating in a way that hadn't been seen before. For generations, stock markets were real places where traders got together to buy and sell shares face-to-face. Then the NASDAQ opened, and everything changed. Though it wasn't widely recognized at the time, this plucky new-style stock exchange would shift the way markets traded, and vastly improve the speed and accuracy of trades.

Taking Over

NASDAQ is the largest (by number of companies) and fastest-growing stock exchange in the United States, and it trades more shares in a day than any other U.S. exchange. On May 26, 2016, total trading volume topped 1.6 billion shares.

When it first launched in February 1971, the NASDAQ hosted only 250 companies. Its first claim to fame: the NASDAQ opened as the first fully electronic stock market in the world. Through the turbulent 1970s, the exchange began to grow, and it became a beacon for young computer-based start-up companies, many of which disappeared as fast as they came on the scene. By the 1980s, computers were gaining ground, and two groundbreaking companies issued IPOs, a powerful indication of what was to come. Those two companies, Apple Inc. (1980) and Microsoft Corporation (1986), changed everything, each eventually becoming (at least for a time) the biggest corporation in the world.

The exchange hit a milestone in 1996, when its trading volume finally exceeded 500 million shares per day. Suddenly, the NYSE wasn't the only exchange hosting successful, respected companies. Now the NASDAQ has grown into a full-fledged stock market, listing about 3,200 corporations, and it's destined to keep growing. Out of all the U.S. stock markets, the NASDAQ (which is now officially known as the NASDAQ OMX Group) hosts the most initial public offerings (IPOs), and it is drawing in more companies all the time.

The NASDAQ is attractive to new and growing companies primarily because the listing requirements are less stringent than those of the NSYE, and the costs of listing can be considerably lower. Not surprisingly, you'll find a lot of technology and biotech stocks listed on this exchange, as these types of companies typically fall squarely in the aggressive growth category. In fact, the NASDAQ boasts more than $9.5 trillion total market value, most of that coming from the technology sector. To catch a glimpse of the companies listed on this exchange, take a look at the NASDAQ Composite, a comprehensive stock index that follows all of the corporations listed there (more on that in the NASDAQ Composite chapter).

The NASDAQ is a dealer market, which means its securities are traded by dealers through telephone and computer networks as opposed to being facilitated by specialists on a physical exchange floor.

DEALER MARKET

Unlike the auction-style trading floor of the NYSE, the NASDAQ works with more than 600 securities dealers known as market makers. Market makers do just what it sounds like they do: they create a market for securities. They even put up their own capital in order to provide a liquid market for investors, making it easier for them to buy and sell shares.

Though the name seems to imply that market makers are individual traders, most are big investment companies (at least on the NASDAQ). That's how they're able to keep a large supply of stocks on hand that can be sold when orders are placed. There's a lot of overlap in the companies that these market makers keep in inventory, which leads to robust competition. Because the exchange is fully computerized, market makers don't conduct business face-to-face, or even over the phone. All trading on the NASDAQ is done electronically.

A Deal's a Deal

When a market maker enters a bid or ask price for a particular stock, he has to buy or sell a minimum of 1,000 shares at that published price. After that's accomplished, he can close out that "market," and put in a new price for that stock.

These market makers compete against one another to offer the best bid and ask prices (or quotes) over the NASDAQ's complex electronic network, which joins buyers and sellers from all over the world. In fact, market makers must offer firm bid and ask prices, creating what's called the "two-way" market (in FINRA terms). In other words, market makers have to trade shares at the bid and ask prices they have quoted. Between the two amounts is the bid-ask spread, the mathematical difference between the two quotes, and the spot where these market makers can make a lot of money. To level the playing field for investors, market makers are legally required to fill market orders at the *best* bid or ask price for the customer.

A NASDAQ DEAL

Let's walk through the way a deal on the NASDAQ goes down. It starts with the market maker entering bid and ask prices, say a bid/ask of $85.20/$85.25 for a share of Netflix. That means the market maker will buy shares for the bid price of $85.20 and sell shares at the ask price of $85.25. The difference between those bid and ask prices is five cents per share, and that represents the market maker's profit, known as the spread.

This looks a little different from the investor's perspective. With those quotes, an investor looking to sell at the current market price would receive $85.20 per share, while an investor looking to buy would pay $85.25 per share.

THE OTC MARKET

Murky, Shark-Infested Waters May Hide Buried Treasure

The over-the-counter market, or OTC market, includes securities known as "unlisted stock." This unlisted designation means these stocks are not traded on the traditional stock exchanges like the NYSE or NASDAQ. Instead, securities bought and sold on the OTC are traded by individual broker-dealers, professionals who deal directly with each other via the Internet or by phone.

Buying OTC stocks is very different than buying stocks traded on the major exchanges, in that there is no central exchange for them where buyers and sellers are matched up. Rather, you can only get shares through a market maker, who must actually keep an inventory of shares for sale.

To buy OTC shares, you typically must enlist the services of a broker who is willing to work with the OTC market, and not all of them will. Then your broker has to contact the market maker for the security you want to buy. The market maker will name his ask price, which is the amount he's willing to accept for the shares. To sell OTC shares, the process works the same way: Your broker would contact the market maker to learn his bid (or offering) price. Bid and ask quotes appear on the OTCBB, the Over-the-Counter Bulletin Board, so that investors can monitor them.

The process seems simple, but it's fraught with risk. Companies traded on the OTC market are usually too small to be listed on a formal exchange, and reliable information about them can be very hard to find. On top of that, OTC shares are not liquid, so it may be very hard to sell them when you're ready to do so.

OTCBB

The OTCBB, or Over-the-Counter Bulletin Board, lists OTC securities that don't quite make the cut for inclusion on a major exchange due to their listing requirements. On the OTCBB, there are no listing requirements except one: Companies listed on the OTCBB must be registered with the SEC, and thus be subject to its reporting requirements. Corporations that are late with SEC filings can be kicked off of this exchange, and moved down to the pink sheets, an unregulated electronic OTC market. If they catch up and remain current, they can come back to the OTCBB.

Part of NASDAQ, But Not NASDAQ

The OTCBB is owned and run by NASDAQ, but it is not part of the NASDAQ exchange. In other words, shares listed on OTCBB are *not* listed on NASDAQ. Unscrupulous market makers may not make that distinction clear, and use the NASDAQ name to make an investor feel more secure about a stock he's thinking of buying.

Owned and operated by NASDAQ, the OTCBB is a fully electronic system with real-time quotes, the most current pricing information, and the most current trading volume for all of the OTC stocks. Keep in mind that the most current information is based on the last time the stock was traded, which may have been a while ago. Securities listed here have the suffix "OB" attached to their ticker symbols, making it clear that they are only traded over the counter.

Technically, the stocks here are quoted, not listed; the term "listed" implies that a security trades on a major exchange.

Buying stocks listed on the OTCBB is inherently more risky than buying stocks quoted on the major exchanges for two very important reasons:

1. This is a much smaller market, and is therefore less liquid. In practical terms, this means investors may have a very hard time selling these stocks.
2. Because of the low liquidity, stocks trading over the OTCBB have much larger bid/ask spreads, which eats into investors' returns.

From the investor's perspective, buying stocks that trade on the OTCBB is like any other stock purchase: You simply call your broker and tell him what you want to buy. From there, the broker contacts the market maker, who quotes the current ask. If you've placed a market order (an immediate order filled at the current price), that ask will be the price for the stock you're buying, and the trade will go through right away. Because this is such a thinly traded market, consider using limit orders (a special order to be filled at a predetermined price) when trading here, because they offer at least some built-in price protection.

PINK SHEETS

To be listed on the pink sheets, an unregulated offshoot of the OTC market, all a company has to do is fill out a form (Form 211, to be specific) and file it with the OTC Compliance Unit. All the form asks for is some current financial information, supplied by the company. That's it.

There are only a few reasons why a company would be traded here:

- The company is very small and can't afford to be listed on a more prestigious exchange.
- The company has been kicked off a major exchange due to noncompliance.
- The company isn't real, and its shares are part of a money-making scam.

Some companies give their market maker access to more detailed financial information, including open access to their accounting books. That makes it easier for the market maker to figure out the right stock price. But since corporations are not required to do that, many of them don't. They don't have to share any information with potential investors, and they also do not have to file any reports with the SEC, and so investors will have a hard time getting reliable or verifiable information before investing.

Ticker Trivia

"Pink sheets" are so called because the trading information used to be printed on pink paper.

On top of that, companies trading over the pink sheets are usually very small, and their shares are typically held by only a few people. With such a limited market, it can be very hard for investors to sell their shares when they want to.

So what makes pink sheets stock attractive to investors? For one thing, share prices are usually very low, often less than $1. With that minimal per-share cost, even tiny movements in price can bring sizeable returns. For example, say you buy 100 shares of stock in Tiny ABC Inc. for $1 per share, a total investment of $100. A few weeks later, the stock goes up by five cents a share, making your investment worth $105 now. That's a 5% return on your investment. The same price movement on a more expensive stock, say one trading for $10 per share, would be barely noticeable.

Delisted Companies Land Here

When a company gets kicked off of a major exchange (like the NYSE), a process known as delisting, it lands on the pink sheets. This happens when the corporation no longer meets the minimum listing requirements, often as a result of an unfortunate financial event that endangers the company's future. Investors who think the company will turn around can scoop up shares on the pink sheets, often at a fraction of its original listed share price.

The real attraction to pink sheet stocks is possibility—the chance that a tiny company will hit it big. In this age of innovation, where the next major breakthrough could come from one guy with a laptop working from his garage, the prospect of getting in on the ground floor of a future Twitter, Amazon.com, or the next big thing is very enticing. Even if the pink list stock never makes it onto a major exchange, it still has the potential to bring enormous returns due to the small initial investment.

Fairly recently, a tiered system was added to the pink sheets trading world to give investors a better idea of just how risky a potential investment may be. The five tiers are aptly named, giving investors crucial information with just a glance.

1. The *trusted* tier contains companies considered trustworthy. These companies adhere to listing guidelines and provide investors with information, and may even report to the SEC.
2. The *transparent* tier includes companies also listed on the OTCBB, which requires regular and current reporting to either the OTC Disclosure and News Service or the SEC. This reporting allows investors to see what's going on with the companies.
3. The *distressed* tier includes companies that aren't quite so forthcoming with current information or have declared bankruptcy.
4. The *dark/defunct* tier contains companies that either haven't filed any information within the past six months (indicated by a stop sign symbol) or gray market companies, which have no market maker and are not quoted on either the OTCBB or the pink sheets (indicated by an exclamation point).
5. The *toxic* tier comes with a skull-and-crossbones warning to indicate securities that have been marked as suspicious. Some may not even be real companies.

Investors who have the stomach for stocks traded on the pink sheets may need to find a willing broker; not all brokers are agreeable to helping clients buy these high-risk securities. Many of these companies are earnestly trying to grow their businesses and will happily share information with agencies and investors alike. But others are flat-out scams, so beware.

FOREIGN EXCHANGES

It's a Small World After All

When American investors see that stock markets overseas are racking up extraordinary triple-digit returns, they want to dive right in and share the profits. Until about fifteen years ago, it was practically unheard of for Americans to directly buy stocks on foreign exchanges. In fact, as recently as 2006, it was very difficult to trade foreign shares. Certain online brokerages (including Fidelity) now offer investors the option to sign up for international trading, allowing them online access to a variety of overseas stock markets. Even though you can buy shares directly on foreign exchanges, it's still not quite as easy as buying on the American exchanges.

Ticker Trivia

The world's first stock exchange opened in Antwerp, Belgium, in 1460.

For one thing, to buy shares on a foreign exchange you first have to convert your money into the local currency, and changes in currency exchange rates can affect your returns. For another, some world markets have a lot less trading volume than the U.S. markets, and that can make it more difficult to find a buyer when you're ready to sell (or find a seller when you want to buy).

In addition, some brokerage firms will not trade on foreign markets directly. Instead they offer investors the chance to buy into foreign ETFs (exchange-traded funds), foreign mutual funds, or foreign stocks traded on the American exchanges, called ADRs (American Depositary Receipts).

The Time Difference

When you invest directly in foreign stocks traded on foreign exchanges, time will be an issue. Whether you use an online broker or a brokerage firm in the country where the stocks are traded, purchases and sales can only be made when those markets are open, in local time.

To counteract those impediments, investors can try to open brokerage accounts in the foreign countries where the stocks they're interested in are traded. For example, to directly buy shares in a company traded on the London Stock Exchange, you can set up an account and work directly with a British brokerage firm. Keep in mind, though, that stocks you buy on a foreign exchange can only be sold on that same exchange, even if the company is listed on other exchanges.

Why go through all the trouble of investing outside the United States? For one thing, though foreign stocks can be more risky for a wide variety of reasons (limited information, political instability, shifting foreign exchange rates, for example), they also offer a wealth of opportunity. In fact, some of the largest companies in the world are based outside the United States, and are headquartered in up-and-coming economies like Brazil and South Korea. On top of that, foreign economies often move differently than the U.S. economy and each other. So when the U.S. economy is entering a down cycle, for example, the economy in Hong Kong could be in an upswing.

Some of the most prominent stock exchanges outside the United States are:

- London Stock Exchange (LSE), in England
- Tokyo Stock Exchange (TSE), in Japan
- Shanghai Stock Exchange (SSE), in China
- Stock Exchange of Hong Kong (SEHK), in Hong Kong
- Euronext NV (ENX), headquartered in the Netherlands
- Mexican Stock Exchange, or Mexican Bolsa (MEXBOL, or BMV), in Mexico

While these exchanges are among the world's largest, and hold the lion's share of market capitalization, there are many more stock exchanges around the world.

Let's take a more in-depth look at some of the biggest world exchanges.

LONDON STOCK EXCHANGE

One of the oldest stock exchanges in the world, the London Stock Exchange (LSE) has roots going back to the seventeenth century, when traders met in coffee houses. In 1973 local exchanges were merged to form what was originally called the Stock Exchange of Great Britain and Ireland, later renamed the London Stock Exchange.

For many years, those exchange members made deals on the trading floor in London, until technology took over. Today, trading on the LSE takes place via computers, processing more than a million transactions every day.

The LSE operates in more than one hundred countries, and offers access to both British and overseas securities to investors around the world. It includes around 350 companies from more than 50 countries.

Officially called the Financial Times Actuaries 100 Index, the FTSE (pronounced "footsie") 100 index is the most widely tracked stock market index in the world. Launched in 1984, the FTSE tracks the 100 largest blue chip companies listed on the London exchange, representing about 80% of the LSE's market capitalization.

Ticker Trivia

Monikers mean a lot in the world of stocks, conveying a wealth of information in very few words. For example, "blue chips" refers to the most well-established, prestigious corporations. Penny stocks, on the other hand, are very small, unknown companies whose shares may trade for literal pennies.

Prominent corporations listed on the LSE include GlaxoSmith-Kline, Unilever, and Barclays.

TOKYO STOCK EXCHANGE

The Tokyo Stock Exchange was first opened in 1878, trading precious metals and government bonds. Stocks joined the party in the 1920s. Interrupted by World War II, the exchange reopened in May 1949, and by 1989 (right before the big crash) its total market value topped $4 trillion. Now the exchange lists nearly 2,000 firms, including some of the most successful companies in Japan.

You can easily track the TSE by watching the Nikkei 225 Stock Average, usually referred to simply as the Nikkei (pronounced "knee-kay"), a stock index that tracks the ups and downs of the Japanese stock market. It includes 225 blue chip stocks, all headquartered in Japan. The Nikkei is similar to the S&P 500 Index in the United States, which tracks the share price activity of 500 of the largest corporations on the market (to learn more, check out the S&P 500 chapter). Another way to gauge the Japanese market is with the TOPIX (Tokyo Stock Price Index). TOPIX, which launched in 1968, covers about 70% of the Tokyo Stock Exchange, tracking primarily large-cap stocks (stocks with market capitalization of at least $10 billion).

Trading with ADRs

Americans can participate in foreign stock markets in a few different ways. Among the simplest is through the use of ADRs (American Depositary Receipts). Many foreign stocks are listed as ADRs on U.S. stock exchanges (primarily NASDAQ and OTC), giving U.S. citizens a quick and easy way to add foreign holdings to their portfolios.

Unlike most other major exchanges, the TSE has two trading sessions per day. The morning session, called "zenba," is open from 9:00 A.M. to 11:30 A.M.; the afternoon session, called "goba," runs from 12:30 P.M. to 3:00 P.M. Stocks listed on the TSE trade in 1,000-share blocks, and virtually all trades are executed electronically.

The TSE has a tumultuous history. In 1980, the Nikkei was plodding along at 6536, but then Japanese stocks soared. By December of 1989, the index had quintupled to 38916. But in the 1990s, fortune ran the other way, and the Nikkei (along with the TOPIX) took a nosedive. In March 2003, the index plunged below 8000, and continued to follow a rollercoaster-like path over the next decade. In the first half of 2016, the Nikkei bounced around between 15000 and 17000. To limit market volatility, the TSE halts major declines through circuit breaker rules, similar to those used on the NYSE.

Companies listed on the TSE include big names like Honda, Toyota, and Kikkoman.

SHANGHAI STOCK EXCHANGE

Originally opened in the 1860s, the Shanghai Stock Exchange (SSE) was shut down by the Communist Party in 1949. In 1990, the exchange opened again, ushering in a new age for the Chinese economy, one heralded by wild swings, with both market run-ups and crashes.

Unlike other stock exchanges around the world, the SSE operates as a nonprofit organization. It's administered by the CSRC (China Securities Regulatory Commission), and is prone to excessive government oversight. Most of the major companies listed in this exchange used to be state-run companies, including insurance companies and banks. In order to qualify for listing on the SSE, a company has to be in business and earn profits for at least three years.

The SSE, which is the largest stock exchange operating in China, lists two different types of shares: A shares and B shares. A shares are quoted only in Chinese currency, the yuan. They represent stock in companies based on the Chinese mainland. Until fairly recently, only citizens of mainland China could buy A shares. However, approved foreign investors, designated as QFII (qualified foreign institutional investors) are now allowed to purchase them through a special highly regulated system. B shares are open to both foreign and domestic investors, and these shares are quoted in other currencies, like U.S. dollars. Every stock on the SSE trades in both A and B shares.

The main index tracking the Shanghai Stock Exchange is the SSE Composite. This measure is expected to mirror the overall Chinese economy as more state-run companies go public. In 2015, the SSE cycled through majestic highs and painful lows, displaying extreme volatility despite focused government intervention. One reason for those very wide swings was the extremely high proportion of margin trading (when investors borrow against their holdings to buy shares on credit), which involved trillions of yuan (Chinese currency). Another reason was the heavy hand of the Chinese government, which exercised its power even as it attempted to offer freer access to foreign institutional investors.

Companies listed on the Shanghai Stock Exchange include Air China, Bank of China, PetroChina, and Tsingtao Brewery. Though some inroads have been made that allow certain foreign investors to buy Chinese stocks, individual foreign investors can more easily invest in these shares using the Stock Exchange of Hong Kong.

STOCK EXCHANGE OF HONG KONG

The Stock Exchange of Hong Kong was established in 1891. Today, the exchange is primarily driven by the country's highly respected and sophisticated financial services industry. Hong Kong has an intimate relationship and trading partnership with China; its exports to that country alone top $300 billion annually, which amounts to nearly 60% of Hong Kong's total exports. The exchange mimics that pattern, with Chinese companies making up more than half of the stocks trading there.

Hong Kong operates as a "special administrative region" created by the central Chinese government to allow the small nation to operate basically the same way it had under the former British rule. For investors, this distinction is crucial, because the Stock Exchange of Hong Kong operates with autonomy in a capitalist country that is governed by a limited democracy (as opposed to China's communist government and socialist economy).

Cross-Boundary Trading

Shanghai-Hong Kong Stock Connect was launched in November 2014 to make it easier for cross-boundary trading between Shanghai and Hong Kong. This development let international investors have more access to the Chinese stock market than ever before.

During the late 1990s, this exchange was able to start listing H-shares of large Chinese state-owned companies (the H-share designation simply indicates Chinese stocks traded on the Stock Exchange of Hong Kong, in Hong Kong dollars). This is actually the largest market for Chinese equity securities. Today, the stock of nearly 600 companies based on mainland China can be traded on the Hong Kong exchange.

The most important index connected to the Hong Kong exchange is known as the Hang Seng. This market cap–weighted index includes the forty biggest corporations traded on the exchange.

Companies trading on the Stock Exchange of Hong Kong include Bank of East Asia, Air China, and Hong Kong Television Network.

EURONEXT

Headquartered in the Netherlands, Euronext is a cross-border exchange, and the first Pan-European securities exchange. Euronext was born in 2000 by merging the Paris, Brussels, and Amsterdam exchanges. Then in 2002, the Portuguese stock exchange was added, followed later by a London securities exchange (but not *the* London Stock Exchange).

In April 2007, Euronext merged with the NYSE Group to form NYSE Euronext. And by 2008, the combined exchange listed almost 4,000 securities with a total market capitalization of more than $30 trillion.

When Intercontinental Exchange (ICE) bought NYSE Euronext in 2013, the two powerhouses were split once again. Still, Euronext remains one of the largest exchanges in the world. In June 2014, Euronext launched its own IPO, and once again became a standalone entity.

The Euronext exchange system opened up the European stock market, allowing companies to list their securities in multiple markets that fall under a single umbrella. For example, a stock listed on the Euronext Paris exchange can also list on the Euronext Amsterdam exchange. To further facilitate trading, they use the euro as the primary trading currency.

Companies traded on the Euronext exchanges include Air France–KLM, Coca-Cola European, and L'Oréal.

MEXICAN STOCK EXCHANGE (MEXICAN BOLSA)

Plagued by vicious drug cartels and rampant government corruption, the Mexican Stock Exchange (or, as it's known locally, la Bolsa Mexicana de Valores) is the second-largest South American exchange. Headquartered in Mexico City, it is the only securities exchange in Mexico.

Business As Usual?

In this culture of corruption, many businesses unabashedly admit to having paid bribes, and businessmen simply take the dishonest system in stride; it's just a normal cost of doing business. In the rare instances when a corruption case actually makes it to court, there's an 80% chance it won't result in a conviction.

Considered an emerging market, the Mexican economy has been going strong and is predicted to stay on the move upward. Its forward progress continued, though slowed, even during the worldwide recession that characterized the early 2010s. Mexico is among the top ten oil-producing nations in the world, and even with volatile and low crude oil prices, the country has been able to maintain its economic growth.

When it comes to stock market performance, there are two ways to monitor the Mexican market: the MEXBOL IPC Index, which includes a wide range of companies trading on the Mexican stock exchange, and the INMEX index, which tracks the twenty (or so) companies with the largest market capitalization. Foreign investors should factor in the country's gross domestic product (GDP) when considering investments in any securities listed on the Mexican Bolsa. As agriculture contributes greatly to the GDP, paying attention to that economic sector offers additional insights into the company's overall economic health.

The future of Mexican industry, though, seems to be in manufacturing. The country has rapidly risen to superstar heights in this arena, largely due to free-trade agreements and relatively low labor costs.

Companies traded on the Mexican Stock Exchange that American investors may be familiar with include Wal-Mart de Mexico (WMMVY) and Coca-Cola FEMSA (KOF), which is the world's biggest Coca-Cola bottler.

INTERNATIONAL INFLUENCE ON THE U.S. STOCK MARKET

The Butterfly Effect

Terrorist attacks in Belgium, civil war in Syria, financial devastation in Greece, economic slowdowns in China—all of these global events have a large (and sometimes lasting) impact on the U.S. economy and the U.S. stock market. That's how the butterfly effect—a theory explaining how small causes bring large and sometimes unexpected effects—hits the world of finance.

When exports and international sales drop off, the stock market reacts. When oil prices plummet or skyrocket, American corporations see the impact in their stock prices. As the world shrinks, thanks to advancements in communications technologies and international trade deals (like NAFTA) events in other countries affect the U.S. stock market more than ever before.

One important reason for the increased impact is the rise of multinational corporations (MNCs). With operations overseas, these companies can be directly affected by international events. For example, a U.S. corporation with manufacturing plants in Japan could have its operations disrupted by a tsunami. What affects the host country also affects the American corporation with holdings there.

International trading also affects U.S. stock prices. U.S. shares trade on markets all around the world. And because of time differences, there's always a market open somewhere. Because of that, U.S. stocks can be traded twenty-four hours a day, seven days a week, and that has a clear influence on U.S. stock prices.

MULTINATIONAL CORPORATIONS

Multinational corporations (MNCs) are exactly what they sound like: companies that have operations running in more than one country. Based in a home country, these usually large enterprises keep factories and offices in multiple nations, which adds a lot of complications to their corporate structure.

Since every country has its own set of laws, customs, and regulations, a company operating in more than one country needs to bring in teams of lawyers and managers to make sure they're correctly and properly following local rules. As laws everywhere are subject to change any time, multinational corporations have to pay close attention to events in the nations where they have operations and adapt as necessary.

MNCs in America

In addition to American corporations having operations in other countries, many foreign corporations maintain offices or plants in the United States. Examples include Toyota, Nestlé, and GlaxoSmithKline.

A lot of American corporations maintain overseas operations, companies like Coca-Cola, Wal-Mart, and Apple. This setup gives American investors the chance to invest in overseas operations through companies headquartered in the United States. In fact, several U.S.-based companies bring in more than half of their revenues from their foreign business activities.

From an investor's standpoint, this has both benefits and drawbacks. Benefits include things like access to larger markets and tax advantages, both of which may have an immense impact on a company's profitability. One of the important drawbacks is political risk: the chance that a country in which the corporation operates will undergo political or economic changes that have a negative impact on the MNC's profits. Political risk encompasses all manner of issues, from government coups to added financial restrictions to corruption, and any of these can attack a corporation's bottom line.

GLOBAL MARKETPLACE

Whether or not American companies maintain foreign offices or manufacturing plants, they still can participate in the global marketplace. Throughout the world, people gobble up new (at least new to them) American products as fast as corporations can export them. That's why you can visit a Disney theme park in Paris or Tokyo, or buy a Starbucks grande skim latte in seventy countries around the world, from Australia to China to Chile. As American corporations enter new markets and global sales increase, stock prices can rise right along with them.

At the same time, recessions, depressions, and slowdowns in overseas economies now have increasing impact on U.S. companies. For example, a change in Chinese currency valuation led to a drop in the price of Apple shares; since China is Apple's second biggest world market, that move had a big negative impact on the American tech giant's business and its stock value.

A CLOSER LOOK AT CHINA'S IMPACT

As the second-largest economy in the world, China, with its voracious appetite for raw materials and other commodities, has an enormous impact on other countries and their stock markets, and the United States is no exception.

For example, as the standard of living in China changed dramatically, their hunger for Western products became ravenous. Demand for everything from cars to movies to iPhones created a huge new market for American companies. This fundamental shift marked a permanent change for the global economy; once the way people live changes like this, it affects their spending habits going forward.

But when the economy of this giant nation starts to weaken, as it did beginning in 2015, the rest of the world starts to get nervous. And because China is one of the United States' primary partners in trade, accounting for 15% of total trade including $8 billion of American exports every month, a slowing Chinese economy signals a potential slowdown for the U.S. economy as well. Corporations that sell products and services to the Chinese market will see those sales drop dramatically, causing a negative impact on their bottom lines and their stock prices.

Ticker Trivia

During the U.S. financial crisis in 2008, China picked up the tab for a huge chunk of America's debt, making it our country's biggest creditor. According to the United States Department of the Treasury, as of February 2016, Mainland China alone holds more than $1.2 trillion in U.S. debt, and that doesn't even include the U.S. debt holdings of Taiwan and Hong Kong.

BULLS AND BEARS

There's a Reason the Stock Market's a Zoo

The drama of stock market activity makes headlines every day. In many of those headlines, you'll see one of two iconic words: "bull" and "bear." One of those words excites investors and spurs rallies, and the other invites fear and caution, and leads nervous investors to cash out. In Wall Street lingo, bulls represent markets on the rise, and bears signify market slowdowns.

Whether the market is characterized as "bull" or "bear" depends mainly on the prevailing direction of stock prices, but that is not the only factor in play. Other issues that contribute to bull and bear markets may include:

- Investor emotions
- Economic ups and downs
- Supply and demand
- Global conditions

What defines a bull or bear market is time. Long-term market performance determines which animal defines the market, rather than quick spikes or dips that last only a few days or weeks.

SECULAR MARKETS

A market cycle that lasts for many years is called a secular market, regardless of whether it's operating in bull or bear mode. Secular markets last anywhere from ten to thirty years, often brought on by demographic shifts (like the rise of the baby boomers), major changes in technology (like mobile devices), and significant global events (like wars). In a secular bull market, investors will see above-average returns. In a secular bear market, returns will fall below average.

Ticker Trivia

During a secular market, investor sentiment can temporarily sway in the opposite direction, but will then swing back toward the predominant pattern. This brief interruption does not change the characterization of the secular market trend.

Secular bull markets are associated with record highs, extreme investor confidence, and market bubbles. Secular bear markets are characterized by fearful investors, reduced investing and increased savings, undervalued stocks, and record low stock prices.

Since the crash of 1929, the U.S. stock market has experienced both types of secular markets.

From 1929 through 1949, investors remained wary. With minimal activity, that secular bear market brought minimal returns to those still investing. Suddenly, sentiment shifted and market activity picked up.

In 1950, the market changed course. This launched the longest secular bull market in American history, which finally came to an end in 1968. Though the market did see some short-term downturns during that eighteen-year period, returns averaged 11% over that time span.

The war in Vietnam, inflation, global upheaval, high interest rates, and stagflation (a time of slow market growth and high unemployment accompanied by high inflation) marked the next secular bear market, which ran from 1968 through 1982. Those brave enough to invest in the stock market were rewarded with disappointingly low returns.

In 1982, though, the market took a turn toward the bull. With the Dow returning, on average, nearly 17% annually during this bull market, investors were flying high. Interest rates were down, but corporate profits were soaring, and so were their share prices. This exuberant market lasted until 2000, when the dot-com bubble burst.

When the market crashed in 2000 following the implosion of the dot-com bubble, it set off a secular bear market that resulted in crippling losses. The NASDAQ Composite index, comprised primarily of tech stocks, saw a devastating 78% drop in value. And the average annual rate of return on stock investments during this eight-year bear market, -6.2%, still makes investors shudder.

Some analysts believe that 2009 marked the beginning of the next bull market, others say it didn't truly kick in until 2013. Overall, the period has seen consistent growth, and the Dow has seen higher than average positive returns—including several record highs.

BULL MARKET

Bull markets don't last forever, though it may feel that way in the middle of one. During a bull market, investors expect that stock prices will continue to go up. That can lead to more risky buying behavior, as investors look to reap "surefire" rewards.

Americans have seen three major bull markets since World War II. The first began in 1950 and lasted through 1968, and the markets increased by 11%. The next great bull run began in 1982 and lasted through 2000, breaking one record after another as the Dow and the NASDAQ hit all-time highs again and again. The NASDAQ really soared during this great bull market, shooting up 185% between November 1997 and March 2000 . . . a period when the Dow increased 40%.

The Dow Sets New Records

Back in 1982, the Dow Jones Industrial Average (a calculated index based on the value of a basket of stocks) first broke 1000, and things only sped up from there. By 1990, the Dow topped 3000, only to pass 4000 five years later. And by the end of 1995, the index skated past 5000, and hit 8000 by July 1997. By March 1999, the Dow hit a jaw-dropping 10000 followed by a record close of 11722.98 on January 14, 2000.

These market highs continued to come despite economic catastrophes like the Asian market crisis of 1997. And it was during this time that U.S. Federal Reserve Chairman Alan Greenspan uttered his seminal phrase, "irrational exuberance." These cautionary words fell right in the middle of this bull market, and would ultimately prove true when the dot-com bubble finally burst in March 2000, and that great bull market officially ended.

After a couple of years on the downside, the U.S. stock market rebounded starting in October 2002. On October 9, 2002, the Dow was at a new low of 7286. That nearly doubled in just five short years, when the Dow closed at 14165 on October 9, 2007.

Since 2009, the United States has been in another bull market, characterized by consistent growth and average 18% increases in the

Dow and more record highs. As of May 2016, we were still enjoying a bull run. How long it may last is hard to tell.

BEAR MARKET

In a bear market, stock prices fall steadily for a sustained period of time. The technical definition of a bear market is at least a 20% decline in any of the major market indexes (like the Dow or the NASDAQ Composite) that lasts for at least sixty days.

That downward trend leads investors to believe prices will continue to fall for the long haul, so they begin to sell stocks rather than buy stocks.

Increased sales coupled with decreased purchases drive stock prices down further, perpetuating the bear market. Over the long-term, this can affect the corporations themselves, possibly leading to lower profits, and even losses and layoffs. Not surprisingly, bear markets are closely linked with weak economies.

Ticker Trivia

Market corrections aren't the same as bear markets. Though a market correction may be just as steep as a bear market, a correction lasts less than two months. Bear markets last longer.

Since 1929, the United States has weathered more than twenty-five bear markets. The average loss hovered around 35%, and they lasted, on average, for less than one year each. Some, of course, have been much worse than that, such as the extended bear market that dragged from 2000 to 2002, where we saw a 50% decline in market value. And on the heels of the housing bubble burst in 2007, a seventeen-month bear market resulted in a 56% decline in the S&P 500.

CIRCUIT BREAKERS

After the disturbing downturns in 1987 and 1989, the NYSE put "circuit breaker" rules in place to stem massive declines before they can snowball into crashes. The latest version of these rules, approved by the SEC and implemented in 2013, calls for trading halts based on very specific events affecting the S&P 500 Index (a measure of the biggest corporations trading on the stock market).

- A Level 1 halt kicks in when the S&P 500 drops by 7% before 3:25 P.M. on a trading day. A Level 1 halt lasts for fifteen minutes.
- A Level 2 halt comes into play with a 13% decline of the S&P 500, again if the drop occurs before 3:25 P.M. It also lasts for fifteen minutes.
- Level 1 and Level 2 halts can only happen once a day each, but a Level 1 halt can be followed by a Level 2 halt if the index declines further once trading resumes.
- A Level 3 halt is the most serious; it suspends trading for the rest of the day. That happens when the S&P 500 decreases by 20% at any time during the trading day.

BUBBLES

Don't Pop the Champagne Just Yet

When it comes to the economy, bubbles grow to unsustainable size and then burst. They start out as pockets of swift expansion and prices soar when everyone wants in, then the expansion suddenly tails off, and prices plummet during a panicked frenzy of selling. When a bubble bursts, it sometimes snowballs into a full market crash.

These bubbles can form in the overall economy, or they can appear in portions of it, from entire markets to market sectors and all the way down to individual securities. What they all have in common is asset prices that are significantly higher than their true worth. Financial experts coined the phrase "asset price bubble" to describe the phenomenon.

Though seasoned analysts may be able to spot a bubble from the inside, these economic events are often identified only after the bubble has popped.

Ticker Trivia

The first big economic bubble took place in Holland back in the 1630s, when tulip prices rose 2000% before crashing back down in 1637.

BUILDING A BUBBLE

Though the core of a bubble comes from overinflated asset prices with no basis in reality, the events that spur the irrational price hikes are very real. Bubbles can be set off by things like shifting interest rates (like in the U.S. housing bubble), free-flowing credit (also a major factor in the housing bubble), and new innovative developments in technology (as were seen throughout the dot-com bubble). Once people start to catch the new fever, the bubble begins its tenuous growth, and prices take baby steps upward.

Prices begin to gather momentum as more people jump on the bandwagon. Media coverage increases, which draws in even more excited participants hoping to get in on this strike-it-rich opportunity.

High on the quickly climbing prices, investors throw caution to the wind and enthusiastically pour more money into the mix, sending prices to exorbitant levels. This was seen at the peak of the dot-com bubble, when the tech stock portion of the NASDAQ hit levels that were higher than the GDP of some countries. With market values out of control, traders, advisors, and talking heads cook up reasons to justify continued investment.

As prices reach their tipping point, smart investors realize it's time to get out and they try to clear profits before everyone else catches on. But when markets act in irrational ways, it's virtually impossible to make a clean getaway. All it takes is the tiniest pin to pop a bubble, immediately and forever halting its expansion, and setting off its inevitable unraveling.

A Return to Reality

Despite the fact that fortunes get decimated when asset price bubbles burst, a market correction also brings balance back to the system. In other words, prices return to realistic levels that reflect the intrinsic value of the assets.

Now mass panic sets in. The bubble bursts as prices plummet even faster than they rose. Investors desperately try to sell off their over-priced assets before they're fully worthless. With more sellers than buyers, prices hit rock bottom. Individual and institutional investors, whole markets, even whole economies can collapse once the bubble has popped.

THE NEXT BUBBLE?

Investment and economic analysts attempt to forecast the next bubble before it blows up, and they also try to pinpoint the moment right before the burst. While some of them are likely to be right, in truth their predictions can be as much guesswork as foresight. Realistically, bubbles are usually defined only after they've popped, meaning that any investment opportunities have already been lost. But that doesn't mean industry insiders can't pick up on signs that market fluctuations are more than just normal movements.

Not all gains in asset prices are unrealistic. Sometimes value truly increases, even in the midst of investor excitement. As for coming out on the right side of bubble timing, it's as likely as winning the lottery: A few very lucky people may get it right, but most investors won't end up hitting it big. How high prices will rise, how quickly they'll inflate, and how long the bubble will last are all highly unpredictable events. But despite the tumultuous rise and fall of stock prices during a bubble, over time, it still pays to participate in the stock market.

DOT-COM BUBBLE

The Internet was just beginning to gain momentum. Personal computers had just started to be a part of everyday life. It was the 1990s, and the technology was so new that no one could predict the ways it would change our world. At the time, the innovations were intoxicating, and so eager investors wanted in. The rush to profit from these innovations spurred the unfortunate creation of the ill-fated dot-com bubble.

The excitement over dot-com companies grew, and share prices increased accordingly. Most of these new dot-com stocks showed up on the NASDAQ, and the value of the exchange grew five times over in just five years.

During that time, IPOs emerged like ants at a picnic. They commanded huge prices from day one, and some of them saw their share prices gain 100% on that very first day. Hundreds of those companies, almost as soon as they went public, garnered billion-dollar valuations. But most of them were not worth even close to what investors were willing to pony up.

Suddenly, some of the biggest tech companies of the time (like Dell) started to sell their stock, and investors began to get very nervous, selling off their tech holdings in a panic. Without the constant

Ticker Trivia

According to legendary investor George Soros, "Stock market bubbles don't grow out of thin air. They have a solid basis in reality, but reality as distorted by a misconception."

inflow of capital, most of those "pop-up" dot-com companies went under and their shares became worthless. And, just like that, billions of investors' dollars simply disappeared.

HOUSING BUBBLE

Newspaper headlines contained words like "crisis" and "collapse" and "bailout," and investors began to panic. In the fall of 2008, the major financial markets in the United States lost nearly a third of their value. As the subprime mortgage fiasco unfolded, it dragged the country's economy down with it. Though the U.S. housing bubble wasn't directly tied to the stock market, its collapse did have a huge impact on stock market behavior.

The story of one of the worst financial crises in American history started before the turn of the millennium, back in 1999. The economy was humming along, and the real estate market was booming. Everyone wanted to buy houses, but not everyone had good enough credit to qualify for mortgages. Until, that is, subprime lending to high-risk borrowers became the new standard.

With horrible credit history, limited income prospects, and minimal (if any) savings to fund a down payment, people were still getting mortgages from greedy predatory lenders. Even worse, those mortgages came with some pretty nasty twists and intricacies that many new borrowers did not understand. These included:

- Interest-only loans, which look good at first glance, but can result in much more expensive mortgages
- Adjustable-rate mortgages, or ARMs, which change not only the interest rate on the loan but also the monthly payments

- Payment-option ARMs, which give the borrower a choice of possible payments, some of which won't actually pay down the loan itself

While the housing market was flying high, these risky loans *seemed* risk-free. After all, it was as easy to sell a house as it was to buy milk, and homes were constantly increasing in value. So borrowers appeared to have equity in their homes because the houses were suddenly worth more. That situation was about to change, but not until a lot of investment banks and investors bet big on a new fad known as mortgage-backed securities (MBS). Basically, an MBS is a bond backed by mortgages, and bondholders get paid as mortgage payments come in. As long as people are paying their mortgages, these securities work.

But very quickly, interest rates on those ARMs reset and payments increased, and suddenly people couldn't afford to make their monthly mortgage payments, so they defaulted on their loans. At the same time, the housing market tanked, and home values plummeted. Millions of proud homeowners found themselves "upside down," owing more on their home loans than those houses were worth. Selling the house would not cover the full mortgage, so they would still owe money, but they would no longer have a house.

Ticker Trivia

The bursting of the U.S. housing bubble had devastating implications around the world, evaporating wealth throughout Europe as international banks were left holding worthless subprime mortgage-backed securities.

The housing bubble had burst. Foreclosures became commonplace, and personal bankruptcy rates skyrocketed. And without incoming mortgage payments to prop them up, the MBS market collapsed and took recklessly irresponsible major investment banks down with it.

Those infamous bank failures on top of the distressed mortgage and housing industries dragged the country into a recession in the winter of 2007, and the stock market dropped along with it. By mid-2008, the Dow Jones Industrial Average dropped to a two-year low, and kept falling. As investors pulled their money out of the stock market in a panic, share prices hit devastating lows.

CRASHES

The Tower of Terror Comes to Wall Street

A crash occurs when the total value of the stock market takes a significant nosedive. This often happens when a bubble bursts and most stockholders try desperately to sell off their shares at the same time. When more people want to sell than buy, prices drop dramatically, and investors begin to incur huge losses.

Not every big drop in total market value is considered a crash, though. Sometimes, stock prices dip because they're simply higher than they should be, and investors suddenly realize that. This kind of dip is called a correction. Corrections differ from crashes in two very important ways: they're smaller drops, and they don't last as long. As scary as corrections may seem to nervous shareholders, they really indicate a return to sensible investing.

Market crashes, on the other hand, can be terrifying. The two worst in American history are the crashes of 1929 and 1987. Other noteworthy crashes are those of 2010 and 2015.

THE CRASH OF 1929

Between the beginning of September through the end of October 1929, the stock market saw an enormous 40% drop. That decline continued until the market hit rock bottom in the summer of 1932, when it was almost 90% down from its former peak in early 1929.

But before that terrible crash, the market and its investors were flying high. After emerging victorious from World War I, Americans were full of confidence and hope, and believed the stock market would make everyone filthy rich. They didn't see any risk, and weren't worried about a downside. So they poured all of their money into the market without asking any questions. In fact, most of them didn't really know how the market worked at all.

Some unscrupulous swindlers took advantage of their optimism, and they joined forces to influence stock prices by trading shares among themselves. They made it look like the prices were going up substantially, a practice colorfully known as "painting the tape." That enticed excited investors to buy, while the swindlers sold for artificially inflated prices and made enormous profits.

In fact, just two weeks before the bottom fell out, the Dow Jones Industrial Average index climbed to 386.10, a height that wouldn't be reached again until 1954. After that peak, the Dow declined steadily, and the pace of the fall began to quicken.

Ticker Trivia

In 1929, the Dow included companies like Chrysler, General Foods, Sears Roebuck & Company, U.S. Steel, and (of course) General Electric.

By Wednesday, October 23, 1929, the Dow had dropped to 305.85, with 6.3 million shares trading. The next day, it opened with a small rally. That rally was gobbled up by a tide of selling, with 12.9 million shares traded. The Wall Street offices couldn't keep up with that volume of trading, and so information lagged far behind the activity of the day. When the market opened the next Monday morning, the Dow opened low, dropped, and closed down 13%.

As the opening bell rang on Tuesday, October 29, the market was flooded with sell orders. Under that pressure, prices fell right away. In the first thirty minutes of trading, 3.3 million shares changed hands. Everyone wanted to sell, accepting whatever bids they could to close out their positions. Damaging losses were widespread, and the Dow dropped to a devastating low of 212.33. On that single day, now known as Black Tuesday, trading volume hit a record 16.4 million shares.

Finally, the panic selling stopped, but stock prices continued to drop. And though there were still some ups and downs, the ensuing bear market lasted through 1932, a year during which the Dow never posted a gain.

THE CRASH OF 1987

It was the largest single-day drop in history. On October 19, 1987, now known as Black Monday, the American stock market lost $500 billion, and the Dow suffered a 22.6% loss in a single trading session.

This sharp downturn came on the heels of rising markets for the first half of the year, leading some conservative analysts to warn of a bubble effect. Despite the valiant efforts of the Securities and Exchange Commission (SEC), investors—even large institutional investors—weren't listening to logic. The drama of hostile takeovers and IPOs excited investors, and stock prices shot up to undreamed of levels.

By the middle of October, the economic forecast was beginning to look bleak: The dollar was down, and the United States was experiencing a large trade deficit. Investors reacted to the dreary news, and the market began to see losses on a daily basis. At the close of trading on Friday, October 16, the Dow posted a 4.6% loss, and investors got even more nervous.

By the time the U.S. markets opened the next Monday morning, the rest of the world had seen similar declines, especially in the Asian markets. When the opening bell on the NYSE rang that day, the Dow began its descent immediately, finally sliding down 508 points.

What followed that dark day was different than the sustained economic troubles of the crash of 1929. The economy didn't plunge into a recession; there was no run on the banks. And the markets made a quick recovery, gaining back about half of their Black Monday losses in just a couple of trading sessions. In fact, it would take only two short years for the Dow to exceed its precrash high.

THE FLASH CRASH OF 2010

Though the direct cause of this momentary crash remained unknown for years, the flash crash of 2010 was marked by a 600-point drop in the Dow and a substantial single-day dive in the S&P 500, a 7% decline that took place in under fifteen minutes on the afternoon of May 6.

That quick drop was matched by an equally speedy recovery, leaving investors and regulators puzzled. In a kneejerk reaction, exchanges canceled more than 20,000 trades that took place during the drop, all deals completed at unusually low prices.

At first, market regulators thought a typo spurred the brief flash crash; that someone had typed in an order incorrectly. This proved untrue. A report released nearly two weeks later included a few guesses, but no primary cause was ever spelled out. Effectively, the flash crash was caused in part by steep declines in specific stocks, including Philip Morris, Procter & Gamble, and Accenture (which dropped all the way down to one penny per share before rebounding).

About a month later, on June 10, 2010, the SEC officially enacted regulations to make sure such an alarming incident couldn't recur. The new rules automatically halt trading activity for any S&P 500 stock if its share price drops more than 10% in five minutes.

In April 2015, U.S. authorities arrested London resident Navinder Sarao in connection with the flash crash of 2010. Sarao was charged with twenty-two crimes, including fraud, for his alleged role in the market manipulation. According to the FBI, Sarao used an automated trading program to pretend to place orders, "spoofing" the market. As of May 2016, the case is still unresolved, and Sarao maintains that he did not intentionally cause the flash crash.

THE FLASH CRASH OF 2015

On August 24, 2015, investors woke to a market panic as the S&P 500 plummeted almost 100 points, a 5% drop, within minutes of the opening bell. This flash crash followed a trend toward selloffs the week before, meaning that investors had a weekend to become even more nervous. So when the Shanghai Stock Exchange Composite Index (SHCOMP) dipped more than 8% on Monday morning, U.S. traders rushed to sell—but no one was buying, and some stocks (shares trading on the major exchanges) literally had no ready market. As more investors and traders trickled into the market, liquidity improved. Throughout the day, the S&P 500 recovered some of its loss, but it still closed down by more than 3%.

PANICS

A Stampede for the Exit

When stock prices start falling fast, investors get caught up in panic selling. A panic can be focused on one company or industry, or hit the market as a whole depending on investor confidence and sentiment. During a panic, investors just want out, no matter how little money they can get for their shares. They trade on emotion rather than information. In the worse cases, panic selloffs results in market crashes.

Most major stock exchanges have some kind of safety net in place to curb panic selling and to give investors time to absorb the fast-flying information. The hope here is that after a brief pause, the market can return to trading more normally. The NYSE, for example, has a set of "circuit breaker" rules in place to halt trading under specific circumstances.

Panic over the fall of a company's share price can spread quickly, like a virus, often infecting a whole industry. And if that virus isn't stopped, it can take down the whole market.

Two Sides of Panic

Though most panics involve selling, panic buying can occur, too. This happens when investors desperately try to get in on a hot stock before its price levels off so that they don't miss out on big profits.

When a company is the initial focus of panic selling, that's usually because something has occurred that makes investors think a company's fundamental value is going to decrease. These events can include an SEC investigation, a scandal, a patent loss, or a big lawsuit. For example, when the Volkswagen emissions scandal made headline news, investors rushed to sell their shares, and the stock price still hasn't recovered.

THREE BLACK DAYS

Devastating days for the financial markets are called black days. These notorious days mark catastrophic drops in market value, as benchmark indexes plunge and investors suffer enormous losses.

The first of these financial disasters came on September 24, 1869, Black Friday. It came about when a pair of infamous investors sought to corner the gold market and failed. That market collapsed, and it dragged the U.S. stock market down with it.

The most notorious black market day occurred in 1929: Black Tuesday. On Tuesday, October 29, 1929, the U.S. stock market tanked, setting off the Great Depression.

On another fateful October day, Black Monday, the Dow dropped by more than 20%. That took place on October 19, 1987, and it was the biggest single-day decline the market ever saw. Unlike other market catastrophes, this one wasn't brought on by a specific definable event.

THE 2008 MARKET DEBACLE

In the beginning of 2007, the titanic investment bank Bear Stearns failed after suffering huge losses when the housing bubble collapsed.

Heavily involved with subprime mortgage investments, Bear Stearns crumbled. Slowly it pulled the rest of Wall Street down with it, though that would take a little while.

It took time for the stock market to react, and the Dow was still climbing to a high of more than 14000 in early October 2007. Then, just two months later, recession hit the United States, and the Dow began its downward slide. By the summer of 2008, the benchmark index fell below 11000.

Another blow came in September, when Lehman Brothers, another giant investment firm, declared the largest bankruptcy that had ever been filed (at the time). It, too, was another losing player in the subprime mortgage market.

The stock market responded dramatically. The very day after the Lehman Brothers announcement, the ill-fated September 15, 2008, the Dow took a nosedive, falling by 499 points.

Three days later, on September 18, the government began to talk about a bailout. That helped the Dow take some wobbly steps up, gaining back 410 points. On the news of a potential $1 trillion TARP (Troubled Asset Relief Program) plan to help avert a complete financial meltdown and an SEC temporary halt to shorting financial company stocks, the market surged forward again. The Dow jumped up another 361 points the next day, to a close of 11388. But that rebound proved fleeting.

After a series of devastating events, including a bank run and problems with the TARP, the Dow fell to a midday low of 7882 on October 10, an unprecedented 3500-point drop from its high on September 19.

THE SEC

Someone Has to Keep the Paperwork Straight

During the Great Depression, Congress passed the Securities Exchange Act of 1934 creating the U.S. Securities and Exchange Commission (SEC). The 1934 act was designed to restore confidence in capital markets by setting clear rules and giving the SEC power to regulate the securities industry. Basically, the SEC watches over the securities industry to make sure no illegal activity takes place. To help with that enormous task, the agency sets strict standards for brokers, investors, and publicly traded corporations. Every corporation whose stock trades on a U.S. exchange must be registered with the SEC.

The agency's main goal is to protect investors by making sure the securities markets remain honest and fair. One way the SEC meets this goal is by making sure publicly traded companies disclose enough accurate information about their business so that investors can make informed decisions. There's a never-ending slew of paperwork and disclosures required of all companies whose stocks trade on the public markets, including annual audited financial statements. In addition to keeping close tabs on publicly traded companies, the SEC also regulates any companies involved with trading and any professionals who offer investment advice.

Ticker Trivia

In addition to its other duties, the SEC oversees trading activity to ensure that investors are getting the appropriate prices when both buying and selling securities.

Most important, though, the SEC is all about you: protecting you from swindles, providing you with reliable information, and keeping your broker in line.

FORMS 10-K AND 10-Q

The SEC requires that all publicly traded companies publish and file regular financial reports. The paperwork (though now it's mainly submitted electronically) provided to the SEC for annual or quarterly reports are called Form 10-K or Form 10-Q, respectively. The point of these hundred-odd-page, very dry reports is to offer investors a complete picture of the company's financial status, which is why successful investors bite the bullet and read them.

A corporation's 10-Q reports are filed for the first three quarters every year, due thirty-five days after the fiscal quarter closes. Instead of a fourth-quarter 10-Q, the corporation files its annual 10-K report. The 10-Q and 10-K reports contain a wealth of information about the company, including an overview of the business, financial statements and disclosures, and a look at corporate management (including things like executive compensation and upcoming or ongoing legal proceedings).

Most investors don't want to read every word in these long reports, especially when they hold stock in many different companies. It's important, though, to at least hit the highlights. On the numbers front, you'll need to do a little math and analysis of your own, such as comparing this year to last, or comparing actual profits to expectations. Reading through the "Management Discussion" section lets investors know what's going on behind those numbers, how things are changing, and what management expects to happen going forward. Finally, the footnotes to the financial statements offer the investors their best chance of sniffing out suspicious or creative accounting practices.

Form 8-K Falls in Between

Sometimes, a major issue comes up that doesn't quite fit into the standard reporting timetable. When that happens, corporations file a Form 8-K to let investors know what's going on in great detail. Events that can trigger an 8-K filing include things like selling off major assets, replacing a CEO, or plans to acquire another company.

ACCREDITED INVESTORS

Not all investors are the same in the eyes of the SEC. Investors with more experience and wealth, called accredited investors, don't need as much protection. Because of that, these investors can participate in high-risk (and highly lucrative) investments that are not available to the rest of us.

To qualify as an accredited investor for SEC purposes (defined in SEC Regulation D, Rule 501), an investor must:

- Earn income of at least $200,000 a year ($300,000 for a married couple) for the most recent two years, and reasonably expect that level of income to continue OR
- Have at least $1 million net worth (individual or joint with a spouse), not including the primary residence (a condition added in 2010) OR

- Be intimately involved as a partner, director, or executive officer in the company issuing the stock

Accredited investors can be people, but they're equally likely to be big companies themselves, like insurance companies or banks. No government agency actually confirms that someone really is an accredited investor; that responsibility lies with whoever is selling the security. Beginning in 2013, the SEC published stricter guidance for people and companies selling restricted investments to accredited investors in an attempt to verify that these investors really are eligible to invest.

Investments open to accredited investors that are not available to the general public include:

- Private equity
- Hedge funds
- Venture capital
- Unregistered securities

Because these securities are not subject to the same disclosure regulations as those issued by publicly traded companies, and because sellers are not required to share specific information with potential investors, these are considered to be high-risk investments.

Get the Facts

The SEC website (www.sec.gov) offers you the opportunity to investigate questionable activities in the stock markets. The SEC also makes available a wide range of public services, including free investment information, up-to-date complaint tracking, and a toll-free information line (1-800-SEC-0330).

EDGAR

EDGAR is like a convenience store for information about corporations. With a few mouse clicks, potential investors can find all the information they need about any company listed on the major exchanges within minutes. The SEC's comprehensive database, known as EDGAR (Electronic Data Gathering, Analysis, and Retrieval), was created in 1984. EDGAR holds a complete database of all corporate reports filed by public companies and complaints filed against the companies all the way back through 1994, more than 20 million documents. This gives individual investors access to the same information at the same time as massive institutional investors.

On the SEC website (www.sec.gov), you can visit this special section and quickly find the information you need to make the best investment decisions.

Inside Details

Through EDGAR, you can find revealing intelligence about any corporation, including details of executive compensation, and who might be planning a corporate takeover.

It's very easy to search EDGAR for information on any company you plan to invest in, making it the best first stop. You can enter either the company name or ticker symbol to begin your search. Using EDGAR, you can gain access to every document a corporation has ever filed with the SEC. Because the wealth of information can quickly become overwhelming, you would do well to focus your review on specific documents. Specific types of filings you should consider searching for include:

- Form 10-Q, quarterly report
- Form 10-K, annual report
- Form 8-K, current report
- Form 11-K, employee stock purchase and savings plans
- ARS, the annual report to securities holders
- DEF 14A, proxy statements

Using EDGAR for the first time can be confusing, so the SEC provides detailed instructions about how to get the most out of your searches. When you run a search, the documents will show up in date order, with the most recent filing appearing first. Using the simple filters at the top of the document lists, you can enter which type of filing you want to see. You can import EDGAR documents directly into Microsoft Excel, which makes it easy to perform a do-it-yourself analysis on the company's financial data.

SEC Takedowns

The SEC's Division of Enforcement does just what the name suggests; it makes sure federal securities laws are followed to the letter. This division investigates possible legal violations, and when it finds that laws haven't been followed, it recommends ways to remedy the situation.

ECONOMIC INDICATORS

What's Driving This Train?

In the classic 1983 movie *Trading Places*, the ragtag team of Billy Ray Valentine (played by Eddie Murphy) and Louis Winthorpe III (played by Dan Aykroyd) outswindle the dastardly Duke brothers by swapping out their advance copy of the orange crop report, a leading economic indicator that holds key information about the orange juice market. The scene moves lightning fast, and in a matter of moments the Duke brothers lose everything while Valentine and Winthorpe amass a great fortune by acting on the real economic indicator. It's a fun movie scene that mirrors trading reality much more closely than you'd expect.

The Eddie Murphy Rule

At the time *Trading Places* came out, the underhanded and highly profitable inside trading move made by Valentine and Winthorpe wasn't illegal. But it is now. In 2010, a special provision called the Eddie Murphy Rule was added to the rules that govern insider trading.

Though the *Trading Places* trade took place in the commodities market, the stock market works the same way: Economic indicators are used by financial forecasters to predict what will happen next, and then traders base buy and sell decisions on that critical information. These indicators are comprised of collections of statistical and survey data, which is bundled into neat numerical packages and released to the public. Unlike the narrowly focused orange crop report in the movie, broad economic indicators are used to forecast sweeping market trends.

INFLATION, DEFLATION, AND STAGFLATION

The state of the economy greatly influences the stock market. Whether the economy is growing, stagnating, or contracting, stock markets react. Three major economic states can and do affect stock prices. These states are inflation, deflation, and stagflation.

Inflation

Inflation is clearly marked by rising prices and falling purchase power. Because every dollar you have is worth less than it was before, it suddenly costs more money to buy the same things. Inflation, when it remains in a manageable 2 to 3% range, is the normal state of the economy. As prices increase, wages, and stock prices tend to follow suit in a healthy economy. But when inflation skyrockets to an unsustainable height, such that it greatly exceeds increases in income, the markets can't compensate. When purchasing power declines too much and too fast, people don't buy as much, and companies start to feel the pinch. Corporations begin posting shrinking profits, causing stock prices to drop.

Runaway Inflation

The U.S. economy saw disastrous inflation in the mid-1970s. While stock market returns hovered at around 6 or 7%, inflation clocked in at nearly double that, rising to more than 13% by 1979.

Deflation

Deflation is an overall decrease in prices. This sounds like it would be a good thing, but it isn't. Typically, deflation is brought on by a widespread reduction in personal or government spending, drying up demand for goods and services. This unfortunate economic state comes with tighter credit policies (making it harder for people and companies to borrow money) and rampant unemployment. As deflation spins out of control, it causes a run of unfortunate and self-sustaining events such as:

- Plummeting corporate profits
- Downsizing
- Plant closings
- Shrinking salaries and wages
- Loan defaults
- Increased bankruptcies
- Decreasing stock prices

This confluence of events can set off panic selling in the stock market, bringing it to the brink of a crash. Prolonged periods of deflation can set off recession or, even worse, a depression.

Stagflation

Stagflation is sort of like the yeti of the economy: It's mythically rare, and not all economists agree on how or when they appear. During a period of stagflation, the economy sees the worst of both worlds. It's a time characterized by high unemployment, slow economic growth, and a declining GDP that occurs at the same time as inflation. Because things that shouldn't be coinciding are indeed happening all at once, it's very hard for the government to take curative steps. For example, anything they can do to address the inflation hurts unemployed citizens, and anything they might do to ease unemployment will send already high prices to the moon.

Oil Spills Over

Sudden spikes in crude oil prices are a main cause of stagflation, as America saw in the 1970s. Unexpected jumps in oil costs affect virtually every industry: When oil forces transportation costs to soar, product prices follow. At the same time, companies desperate to somehow contain costs begin to lay off employees, the precise recipe for creating a period of stagflation.

Each of these economic phenomena has a distinct impact on the stock market. Combined with time and other economic forces, like market trends, their effects on the market can increase or dwindle.

MARKET TRENDS

From terrorist attacks to changing weather patterns, from technological innovations to shifts in consumer tastes, the market reacts to a wide array of factors. Some of these factors are temporary, and some are permanent. From an investor's perspective, identifying major and permanent trends is the key to consistently profiting in the stock market.

Major short-term trends, which last for months or years, can happen in reaction to "black swan" events. For example, terrorist attacks in Europe affect international travel and tourism, which in turn affect the stock prices of companies in the travel industry.

Permanent, or fundamental, changes last forever; there's no going back. The constant flow of information on the Internet gave birth to e-commerce, instant global communication, and limitless entertainment. Streaming video from YouTube and Netflix has made DVD rental shops like Blockbuster Video forever obsolete. Spotify and iTunes transformed the way we listen to and experience music. Companies that don't see and adapt to these seismic changes are destined to disappear.

Beware the Black Swan

Named after the rare bird, black swan events are random, unpredictable, and happen very infrequently, although these days they've become much more common than in times past. The devastating events of September 11, 2001, and the extreme destruction from Hurricane Katrina are two examples of black swan events that had enormous impacts on the U.S. stock market.

Sometimes trends come from consumers themselves, like the boom in gluten-free and dairy-free foods. Even Ben & Jerry's now offers dairy-free ice cream products. The dizzying array of gluten-free cookies, breads, and pastas nearly fill up as much space on the grocery shelves as the wheat-filled products they imitate. Even as recently as five years ago, shopping for gluten-free foods required detective work, usually followed by an arduous trip to a small specialty store to buy exorbitantly priced products.

Market trends can also be shaped by government actions, like interest rate adjustments, new tax laws, or increased spending. International trade agreements can regulate the flow of imports and exports, having a pointed impact on the stock market.

LEADING, LAGGING, AND COINCIDENT

There are three main types of indicators: leading, lagging, and coincident. Each type offers a different way to assess the direction of the economy, which in turn strongly influences the direction of the stock market.

Economic factors that change before the overall economy changes, offering some insight into what comes next, are called leading indicators. As you might expect, these indicators are not always right, but decades of experience show us that they very often offer reliable predictive information for investors. Traders and analysts make their bets based on these indicators of where the economy is headed.

Lagging indicators do just what their name implies: They follow on the heels of a change in the economy or the stock market. Analysts primarily use these indicators to confirm that a change is taking place. One of the most commonly quoted lagging indicators is the unemployment report, because it's a clear measure of the strength of the economy.

Coincident indicators happen right along with changes in the economy. For example, when the economy is strong, people's income increases. Like lagging indicators, coincident indicators help confirm the country's economic health.

THE CONSUMER CONFIDENCE INDEX

On the last Tuesday of every month, at precisely 10:00 A.M., a nonprofit organization known as the Conference Board releases the Consumer Confidence Index (CCI), and the stock market takes notice. Based on surveys of more than 5,000 American households, the CCI gives us an inside look at what average consumers are thinking and feeling about the economy right now, which way they think the economy will move, and what they expect to see six months out. With that very subjective information, analysts and traders get a feel for the prevailing mood. People with confidence in the economy tend to spend more, and so they tend to make bigger purchases (like cars). Historically, the CCI has been a pretty accurate predictor of consumer spending.

HEMLINES, SUPER BOWLS, AND HOT WAITRESSES

Not all economic indicators are carefully calculated and compiled in stuffy rooms lined with super computers. Some of the most popular—and weirdest—indicators look directly at how certain people and events affect the market.

How do hemlines affect the economy? Believe it or not, when hemlines go up and skirts get shorter, the economy and the stock market tend to be on the rise as well. Longer skirts coincide with declining stock prices. Experts believe this lagging indicator holds true because people show off more skin when they're happy and times are good, and that's also when they invest more heavily in the stock market.

Take the Super Bowl indicator, which dates back to 1967, when teams from the NFL and the AFL first battled it out on the field. According to legend, the market soars when an original NFL-based team wins, and it tanks when an AFL-descended team takes the game. This indicator has proven to be 80% accurate since the 1960s.

Then there's the Hot Waitress Index, which gauges the strength of the economy based on the attractiveness of food servers. When there are more good-looking waiters and waitresses, according to this indicator, the economy is struggling. The thinking behind this is that when times are tough, and high-paying jobs (which tend to go disproportionately to better-looking people) are scarce, you'll see more beautiful waiters and waitresses serving your food.

Presidential approval ratings are also rumored to affect the stock market, but not the way you'd expect. As it turns out, the Dow does better when the majority of Americans don't like the President, and his approval ratings sit between 35% and 50%.

STOCK INDEXES

Big Baskets of Corporations

"The Dow closed up 120 points today." "Stocks were mixed at today's closing."

You've no doubt heard these words at the end of newscasts, in radio updates, and at cocktail parties. And while the general idea of these snippets is fairly clear, what stands behind them takes a bit of untangling.

These days in the world of finance, traders, newscasters, and stock analysts use market indexes to track investment performance, and there are literally hundreds of indexes published now.

A stock index is a collection of different stocks; sometimes they're grouped by specific characteristics (a small-cap stock index, for example), and other times they reflect the market itself. Some indexes track very broad sections of the market, while others have a more pointed focus. Using the right indexes as benchmarks will help you gauge just how well, or how poorly, particular stocks are performing—as long as you choose the right index for comparison.

When analysts and brokers are talking about market performance, they'll often refer to an index to measure prices or volume. Three of the most talked about stock indexes in the United States are the Dow Jones Industrial Average (the Dow), the S&P 500, and the NASDAQ Composite, but those are just a few of the hundreds of indexes available for comparison. Other important indexes to follow include the NASDAQ 100, the Russell 2000, and the Wilshire 5000.

THE DOW

A Basket of Influence and Stature

Formally known as the Dow Jones Industrial Average (or DJIA), the Dow is among the most widely recognized measures of American stock market performance. Virtually every report on the U.S. stock market includes the daily movement of this iconic index, even if they don't include any other financial information.

When reporter Charles H. Dow created the index in 1896, it tracked a group of twelve industrial corporations including General Electric, the only company still listed in the index. He published that information in his "Customers' Afternoon Letter," which transformed into today's *Wall Street Journal*. The Dow expanded to include thirty companies back in 1929.

Though the Dow follows the stocks of only thirty U.S. companies, they are among the largest and most influential corporations. All of the stocks that comprise the Dow are considered blue chips, the most prestigious, reliable corporations, and they're all actively traded on the NYSE.

Ticker Trivia

General Electric (GE) has been included in the Dow longer than any other company, though it was actually removed from the index in 1898 and 1901. Added back in 1907, GE has been a flagship member of the Dow ever since. The newest addition to the index is Apple.

Despite its familiar name, the Dow isn't really a true average anymore, and it doesn't include only what most people would consider "industrial" companies. In fact, McDonald's, Disney, Verizon, and Nike all have places in the Dow. The editors of the *Wall Street Journal* decide which thirty corporations make the list, and which get cut. Famous companies that have been dropped from the Dow include Sears, AT&T, and former industrial titan Bethlehem Steel.

POINTS, WEIGHTS, AND THE DOW DIVISOR

When the Dow is talked about in the news, reporters refer to "points" rather than dollars: "The Dow rose by 116 points," for example. While many people just assume that points mean the same thing as dollars here, they don't. Rather, using points is a simpler way to indicate changes in the index. The points are connected to dollars, but it is not a simple one-to-one ratio, and that's largely because of the way the Dow gets calculated, by means of the Dow Divisor.

Dramatizing the Dow

Talking about the Dow in terms of points rather than percentages is a bit of a media trick. It's much more dramatic to say "the Dow is up 500 points" than it is to say "the Dow rose by 3%."

Essentially, the Dow is a price-weighted index. Its value is based on the current share price of each stock in the index. Here's where it gets different, and a little tricky: Rather than just dividing that total value by the number of stocks in the index (like you would for a true average), that total gets divided by a special divisor called the Dow Divisor.

Originally, the Dow Divisor was exactly equal to the number of different stocks in the index, and so was a calculation of a true average. But events over time required a change in the computation. To counteract the impact of occurrences like stock splits, stock dividends, and changes in the makeup of the list, the Dow Divisor was established. For example, if a stock trading for $90 per share underwent a three-for-one split (meaning a stockholder would now have three shares for every one he held before), the share price would artificially drop to $30 per share because of the split even though there would be no real change in the stock's value. The Dow Divisor adjusts for circumstances like this to make sure they don't distort the overall index value.

Because many of the companies on the list have undergone splits and the like, the Dow Divisor has shrunk substantially over time. As of May 2016, the divisor itself was equal to 0.14602. Armed with that information, we can figure out the dollar change in the Dow based on its point change. For example, if the Dow were up 300 points, that number would convert to a dollar gain of approximately $43.81 (calculated as 300 points multiplied by 0.14602).

Ticker Trivia

You can find out how much any individual Dow stock contributed to the overall point change by dividing its change in dollars by the Dow Divisor. For example, say that a stock price dropped by $10. That stock alone would cause the Dow to decrease by 68.48 points ($10 divided by 0.14602).

Because the Dow is a price-weighted index, stocks with higher prices count (or weigh) more than lower-priced shares. That means a stock trading for $100 per share counts five times more than a stock trading for $20 per share. So smaller swings in higher-priced stocks can end up having a bigger impact on the Dow than a relatively huge change in a lower-priced stock.

THE DOW BY NUMBERS

To get a true sense of the historic rise and fall of the U.S. stock market, all you need to do is look back at the Dow. Even a brief glance at some of its most memorable moments will let you see the market's most glorious highs and heartbreaking lows, and how the passage of time affects overall stock prices. In the following table, (I) indicates an intraday (or midday) quote; (C) indicates the quote at market close.

DOW VALUE	QUOTE TIME	DATE
100.25	(C)	January 12, 1906
381.70	(C)	September 3, 1929
230.00	(C)	October 29, 1929
41.22	(C)	July 8, 1932
150.94	(C)	February 4, 1936
500.24	(C)	March 12, 1956
1003.16	(C)	November 14, 1972
2002.25	(C)	January 8, 1987
1738.74	(C)	October 19, 1987
10006.78	(C)	March 29, 1999
11722.98	(C)	January 14, 2000
7286.27	(C)	October 9, 2002

14198.10	(I)	October 11, 2007
6469.95	(I)	March 6, 2009
11205.03	(C)	April 27, 2010
15056.20	(C)	May 7, 2013
18312.39	(C)	May 19, 2015
16459.75	(C)	August 21, 2015
15370.33	(C)	August 24, 2015

With a rich history woven through its ups and downs, the Dow Jones Industrial Average reflects not just the stock market, but the changing moods, landmark events, and economic shifts in the United States and the world.

The Dow Changes Hands

Though the index still bears its iconic name, Dow Jones & Company doesn't own it anymore. In July 2012, the Dow and the S&P 500 came together to become the largest single source of market indexes in a joint venture between S&P Global and the CME Group (owner of one of the world's largest futures exchanges).

S&P 500

Tracking the Rollercoaster

Though this index was launched in the 1950s, its seeds were planted nearly 100 years earlier, when Henry Poor published a groundbreaking work called *History of the Railroads and Canals of the United States*. Despite what that title suggests, this book traced the financial history of the companies involved in those two defining industries, furthering Poor's intent to spread financial information to the public. And it was so successful that Poor began to publish every year.

Inspired by that success, more companies joined the financial tracking game, including two key players: Standard Statistics and John Moody & Company. Standard Statistics soon led the pack, creating an index that at first tracked more than 200 stocks in many different market sectors. That number dropped to ninety because, back then, it was impossible to track more companies—they didn't have computers to do the work.

When Henry Poor's company went under after the big crash of 1929, it was gobbled up by Standard Statistics . . . and the Standard & Poor's 90 Index was born. Back then, this was the only index calculated daily.

The index was finally able to expand when it computerized in 1946. Using an IBM punch card computer, the company gained the capability to track 500 companies, and update their statistics every hour.

Officially launched in March 1957, the Standard & Poor's 500 Index was (and is still) made up of 500 leading companies. The corporations included in this index are intended to represent the broader economy. Changes in the economy can lead to changes in the makeup of the index, as companies are dropped (like Sears, Dell, and Avon) and others are added.

Out of the possible candidates, corporations are chosen for the list by a committee at Standard & Poor's, now one of the nation's leading investment companies. In order to qualify for inclusion in this prestigious list, officially called the Constituent List, companies must meet specific criteria, such as:

- At least $5.3 billion total market capitalization
- Positive earnings over the most recent consecutive four quarters
- U.S. companies only

The S&P 500 is a market-capitalization weighted index, meaning companies with larger market capitalization count more than smaller companies. As a company's share price climbs, it adds more to the overall return of the index. Though the S&P 500 includes only a selection of stocks, many analysts and traders consider it to be a benchmark for the stock market as a whole.

Companies found in today's S&P 500 Constituent List include Apple Inc. (AAPL), ExxonMobil Corp (XOM), and Amazon.com Inc. (AMZN). The most recent additions (as of May 2016) include Acuity Brands, Inc. (AYI) to replace ADT Corporation (ADT), and Global Payments (GPN) to replace GameStop (GME).

Ticker Trivia

The S&P 500 Index is not connected with the *Fortune* 500, though they include many of the same companies. The main difference is that the *Fortune* 500 includes privately owned corporations, while the S&P 500 includes only publicly traded companies.

NASDAQ COMPOSITE

It's Not Just Tech Stocks Anymore

First formed on February 5, 1971, the NASDAQ Composite index includes more than 5,000 stocks, all of which are listed on the NASDAQ exchange. Unlike other stock indexes, the NASDAQ Composite includes other types of equities (like real estate investment trusts, or REITS) rather than only traditional corporate common stock, and not all of the companies included are headquartered in the United States.

Like the S&P 500, the NASDAQ Composite is a market-capitalization weighted index. Because it includes mainly technology and Internet companies, which are businesses that tend to be more volatile, this index can swing pretty widely. However, other industries are represented as well, including finance and banking, consumer products, transportation, and industrial supplies.

Ticker Trivia

The NASDAQ actually maintains several different indexes, including some that are separated by industry, such as banking, biotechnology, computer, industrial, insurance, and transportation.

This index includes companies like eBay (EBAY), Starbucks (SBUX), PayPal (PYPL), T-Mobile (TMUS), 1-800 FLOWERS.COM (FLWS), Norwegian Cruise Line (NCLH), and Facebook (FB).

NASDAQ 100

A Basket of Innovation

A subset of the NASDAQ Composite index, the NASDAQ 100 includes the largest (based on market capitalization) and most actively traded 100 corporations (technically, it now includes 108 companies) listed on the NASDAQ stock exchange. Launched in January 1985, the NASDAQ 100 has become one of the most tracked indexes in the world with its roster of innovative corporations. Though more than half of these companies fall under the tech umbrella (down from nearly 70% back in 2001), other industries are represented as well, like consumer services, healthcare, and telecommunications.

Corporations found in the NASDAQ 100 (as of May 2016) include:

- Bed Bath & Beyond Inc. (BBBY)
- Amazon.com Inc. (AMZN)
- The Kraft Heinz Company (KHC)
- Alphabet Inc. (GOOG)
- Regeneron Pharmaceuticals, Inc. (REGN)
- Tesla Motors, Inc. (TSLA)
- Microsoft Corporation (MSFT)
- Sirius XM Holdings Inc. (SIRI)
- Costco Wholesale Corporation (COST)
- Netflix, Inc. (NFLX)
- Whole Foods Market, Inc. (WFM)

Included in this index, investors will find both U.S. and international corporations listed on the NASDAQ. They remain in the index as long as their average daily trading volume hits at least 200,000 shares. The only companies specifically excluded from the NASDAQ 100 belong to the financial industry.

Over the past several years, this index has become more "grown up," as the companies listed on it evolved. For example, over the five-year period from 2008 to 2013, the average market capitalization of corporations listed on the NASDAQ 100 grew by nearly 400%, from $435 million in 2008 to $1.6 billion in 2013. Now, more than half of the companies included in this index pay regular shareholder dividends, underscoring their success.

RUSSELL 2000

A Look at the Little Guys

Unlike the other indexes we've discussed so far, the Russell 2000 index follows 2,000 of the smallest companies listed on the U.S. stock exchanges. You probably haven't even heard of the overwhelming majority of them, and some of the more familiar listings may surprise you.

Ticker Trivia

The Russell 2000 is home to small-cap corporations, companies with market capitalization between $300 million and $2 billion. In contrast, large-cap companies like those counted in the S&P 500 have market capitalization of at least $10 billion.

Since these companies are less established, make less money, and hold fewer assets than their brothers on the S&P 500 and the Dow, they are more vulnerable to changes in the economy. Because of this, the Russell 2000 is one of the most volatile indexes covering the U.S. stock market.

Created in 1984 by the Frank Russell Company, this market value–weighted index was the first small-cap benchmark for investors. The Russell 2000 cuts across virtually every industry, and focuses on up-and-coming corporations rather than industry leaders. With an average market capitalization hovering at around $1.3

billion, these companies may not seem small. But in the stock market pond they swim in, they're the smallest fish around.

The Russell 2000 includes:

- 1-800 FLOWERS.COM (FLWS)
- Abercrombie & Fitch (ANF)
- Cracker Barrel Old Country Store (CBRL)
- Krispy Kreme Doughnuts (KKD)
- Papa John's (PZZA)
- Smith & Wesson Holding (SWHC)
- Vitamin Shoppe (VSI)

Stocks that trade for less than $1 per share, or that are listed on the pink sheets, are specifically excluded from the Russell 2000.

WILSHIRE 5000

The Whole Enchilada

Though it's not as well known as some of the others, the Wilshire 5000 Total Market Index (TMWX) is the largest index (by market value) in the world.

When it was first created back in 1974, the index was comprised of 5,000 stocks. Don't let the name fool you, though: The Wilshire 5000 now includes only 3,607 corporations, a number that changes quite often along with the number of companies listed on the major stock exchanges. That number has undergone some seismic shifts since its creation, with an all-time high of 7,562 companies in 1998, followed by a steady decline. December 2005 was the last time the index actually included at least 5,000 corporations.

This index keeps track of virtually all of the publicly traded companies that are headquartered in the United States and traded on one of the American stock exchanges, and because of that it's often called the Total Stock Market Index. To be included in the Wilshire 5000, a company's share price has to be easily available, so it doesn't include companies only listed on the Bulletin Board system (also called OTCBB, an electronic trading service for over-the-counter securities).

The Wilshire 5000 is a capitalization-weighted index, which means larger companies count more than smaller ones when the index value is calculated. If a large company's stock has a big price swing, it would affect the index value more than if a smaller company had an even bigger price swing.

MARKET CAPITALIZATION

From XS to XXXL, Size Matters

When it comes to the stock market, size matters. And, here, size is measured in terms of market capitalization, or the market value of all of the company's outstanding shares.

To calculate the market capitalization of a company, multiply the current market price of a stock by the number of outstanding shares. The number of outstanding shares refers to the number of shares that have been sold to the public.

The math is pretty straightforward: A publicly traded corporation that has 30 million shares outstanding that are currently trading for $20 each would have a market capitalization of $600 million. Although there are a few different groupings used to categorize stocks by their capitalization, these categories change over time. For example, back in the 1980s a company with a market cap of $1 billion was considered to be a large-cap corporation; in today's terms, it would fall in the small-cap category. Here's a general rule of thumb you can follow when companies are referred to in terms of their market capitalization:

- Large cap: $10 billion and over
- Mid cap: Between $2 billion and $10 billion
- Small cap: Between $300 million and $2 billion
- Micro cap: Under $300 million

The category a company falls into tells you a lot about its prospects. Large-cap companies, for example, are usually rock-solid businesses you can rely on, but don't have a lot of room for growth.

Small-cap companies, on the other hand, may be poised for explosive growth, but that potential for growth is tempered by lower market share and fewer assets, and the risk that they could easily miss the mark and disappear.

Mega and Nano

To separate out both massive and minute corporations, some analysts add in two more categories: mega cap and nano cap. Mega-cap companies have unimaginable market capitalizations that top $200 billion. On the other end of the scale are the nano caps, extremely tiny companies (at least by market standards) with a market cap under $50 million.

LARGE CAP

Large-cap (also called big-cap) stocks are the biggest players in the stock market, and tend to be the most conservative investments. Though they grab the lion's share of attention on Wall Street, these companies make up just a tiny fraction of the stock market as a whole (based on the number of companies traded). These are the companies you hear about every day.

A large-cap corporation typically has a more solidly established presence and more reliable sales and profits than smaller corporations. Most of the time, larger companies make less risky investments than smaller companies. The trade-off for this stability, though, can be slower growth rates. Many investors hold large-cap stocks for the long term, and for good reason: More than fifty years of historical market returns show that these corporate giants yield only slightly lower returns than short-term investments, and with much less volatility.

In addition, many large-cap corporations offer their shareholders a steady flow of reliable dividends. In terms of investor returns, these dividend streams help balance out the lower growth potential. Plus, it's very easy to find in-depth information about these companies, which helps investors make the best choices when they're deciding where to put their money.

Examples of large-cap stocks include Bank of America (BAC) with a market cap (as of May 2016) of $147.52 billion, and Target Corporation (TGT) with $40.16 billion. In the subcategory of mega-cap stocks, you'll find ExxonMobil (XOM) at $375.28 billion and Microsoft (MSFT) at $394.06 billion.

MID CAP

Mid-cap stocks, as the name suggests, are bigger than small caps but smaller than large caps, and their business stage (where they fall in the continuum between startup and maturity, typically a sustained growth phase) tends to fall right in between the two. Though these companies can offer some distinct advantages to investors, you won't hear much about them. They get much less coverage by analysts and news services than their large-cap brothers, and so these promising companies often get overlooked. That doesn't mean, though, that they aren't worth looking into.

Companies in this grouping are often trying to increase their market share, striving to become more competitive so they can break out of the pack and become the next large-cap company. They can do this because they're successful enough to attract enough financing to expand. That growth effort gives prospective shareholders the opportunity for potentially large gains, if the company takes off.

While they may offer higher returns and more room for sustained growth than large-cap companies, mid-cap companies also come with more inherent risk (though not nearly as much as small- or micro-cap companies). From an investment standpoint, that risk is particularly important to consider. During economic downturns, these up-and-coming corporations may not have the reserves to weather business slumps.

Examples of mid-cap companies include Old Dominion Freight Line (ODFL) with market capitalization of $5.35 billion (as of May 2016), Dick's Sporting Goods (DKS) with $5.40 billion, Staples Inc. (SPLS) with $5.10 billion, and Avis Budget Group (CAR) with $2.60 billion.

SMALL CAP

The small-cap stock category includes many of the small, emerging companies that have survived their initial growing pains and are now enjoying strong earning gains, along with expanding sales and profits. Today's small-cap stock may be tomorrow's leader—it may also be tomorrow's loser.

Small-cap corporations have much more limited resources than mid- or large-cap companies, which makes them very vulnerable to economic downturns. Often, these are very new companies, or companies in new industries, both of which come with a lot of uncertainty.

Overall, these stocks tend to be very volatile and risky, and shares undergo enormous price swings in very short periods of time.

For a lucky few, though, the risk pays off when a small company makes it big.

Ticker Trivia

A safe way of adding small-cap stocks to your portfolio can be through a professionally managed fund, instead of choosing individual stocks. That way, you'll have exposure to potentially explosive profits without the high risk of loss that comes with investing in a specific small company.

MICRO CAP

According to the SEC, micro-cap stocks are defined as shares in corporations with very low market values. Their total market capitalization will be under $300 million. That sounds like a lot of money, but in the world of corporate finance it's barely a drop in the bucket.

In fact, some of these companies are so small that they aren't required to register with the SEC at all. If they have total market capitalization under $10 million and fewer than 500 investors, they don't have to file anything.

Unlike larger corporations, shares in micro-cap companies trade mainly in the OTC (over-the-counter) market, on the pink sheets. And though the NASD (National Association of Securities Dealers) oversees the OTCBB (Over-the-Counter Bulletin Board), this exchange is not part of NASDAQ. Because they're not listed on major exchanges, micro-cap stocks are not subject to listing requirements, like holding a minimum amount of assets or having a minimum number of shareholders. The latter can make it very difficult to sell your shares quickly.

Ticker Trivia

Companies with market capitalization under $50 million are sometimes referred to as nano caps.

Micro-cap stocks are very risky, and their price movement can be extremely volatile. What's more, the micro-cap market is fraught with fraud, schemers, and scams. You may find enticements in your e-mail inbox, with headlines claiming things like, "88% returns in just one day!" The prospect of amazing returns can suck in unskilled investors who are looking to make a killing. If you're planning to dive into the world of micro-cap stocks, make sure you do your homework. You need to be able to tell when you're facing a real goldmine opportunity and when there's nothing backing up the hype.

But not all micro-cap companies are scams. In fact, many of them earnestly want to become solid businesses, and grow into large caps, but that still doesn't mean they will succeed. Often saddled with a lot of debt, negative earnings, and limited assets, these hopefuls can fade away more easily than they can make a sizeable splash.

MARKET SECTORS

Every Slice Has a Different Topping

Investors and analysts alike look for ways to classify stocks. This makes it easier to gauge their stocks' performance, and helps them diversify their portfolios. One of the key ways to classify stocks is by their market sector.

A market sector is a group of industries with a similar purpose. Although people use those two words—"sector" and "industry"—interchangeably, they don't mean the same thing. "Industry" refers to a group of companies that are in the same line of business. Sectors have a broader scope, capturing larger sections of the economy. Indeed, one sector may hold several industries. For example, insurance is an industry, and that industry falls in the financial sector, along with banks and brokerage firms.

Ticker Trivia

In 1900, the railroad sector was by far the biggest, making up almost 63% of the total market. The biggest sector in 2000 did not exist back then: information technology, which comprised about 23% of the 2000 market.

Sectors can be defined in many different ways, but when people refer to market sectors, they're generally referring to these eleven well-defined market segments:

1. Basic materials
2. Capital goods
3. Communications
4. Consumer cyclical
5. Consumer staples
6. Energy
7. Financial
8. Healthcare
9. Technology
10. Transportation
11. Utilities

As you might expect, different sectors flourish whiles others languish in the same economic circumstances. For example, when the economy slows down, the technology sector may decline as the utilities sector gains ground.

OWNERSHIP STATUS

This Is My Company

It's time to take an inside look at stocks, from what they are to all the different types available to what they can mean for your portfolio. Buy-and-hold investors invest in companies that have stood the test of time. Traders take a more active approach to investing, placing more emphasis on stock price movement than on the real value of the company. Regardless of which strategy you apply to your holdings, the same underlying rule applies: Know what and why you're buying (or selling) before you make any trade.

STOCKS ARE PIECES OF A COMPANY

Purchasing shares of stock is like buying a business. That's the way Warren Buffett, one of the world's most successful investors, views it—and his philosophy is certainly worth noting. When you buy stock, you're actually buying a portion of a corporation. If you wouldn't want to own the entire company, you should think twice before you consider buying even a piece of it. If you think of investing in these terms, you'll probably be a lot more cautious when singling out a specific company.

It's important to become acquainted with all of the details of the company you're considering. What products and services does the company offer? Which part of the business accounts for the greatest revenue? Which part of the business accounts for the least revenue? Is the company too diversified? Who are its competitors? Is there a demand for the company's offerings? Is the company an industry leader? Are any mergers and acquisitions in the works? Until you understand exactly what the company does and how well it does it, it would be wise to postpone your investment decision.

Let's say you want to buy a convenience store in your hometown. You've reviewed such factors as inventory, the quality of the company's employees, and customer service programs. In addition to selling staple grocery items, the company also sells lottery tickets and operates a gas pump. The grocery side of the business may only account for a small percentage of the overall revenue. It would be in your best interest to value each part of the business separately in order to get a complete and accurate picture of the company's profit potential. Many companies have traditionally been associated with a specific business, yet may have expanded into totally new ventures. You need to know what businesses a given company operates.

Cigarettes and Wine

The Altria Group, formerly known as Philip Morris, is primarily associated with tobacco products. But the company also profits from its popular wine subsidiary, Ste. Michelle Wine Estates. In addition, the company holds Philip Morris Capital Corporation, which is involved with the financing and leasing of major assets.

Disney, for example, has historically been associated with the Disneyland and Walt Disney World theme parks. The reality is that Disney is also involved in a host of other ventures. Among other things, this multifaceted company has interests in television and movie production, including Touchstone Pictures and Miramax. Disney also has ABC, Inc.; this division includes the ABC television network, as well as numerous television stations and shares in various cable channels like ESPN and SOAPnet.

It should be increasingly clear that making money through investing requires work. The more research and thought you put into your strategy, the more likely you are to reap rewards. Although there are no guarantees in the world of investing, the odds will be more in your favor if you make educated and well-informed investment decisions. When you make an investment, you are putting your money into a public company, which allows you—as part of the public—to become an owner or to have equity in the company. That's why stocks are often referred to as equities.

WHO'S REALLY IN CHARGE?

From the board of directors to the CEO, corporate management involves a lot of decision-makers, and it can be hard to figure out who stockholders should pay attention to on any given day. Because of the way corporations are set up, there's a distance between the people who own the company and the people who run it. To make sure the people running the company act in the owners' (the stockholders) best interests, most publicly held corporations in the United States maintain a two-layer system.

Directly chosen by the shareholders, the board of directors acts as their advocate, monitoring the corporation's operations and management. The head of this group (elected by the group) is the chairman of the board, and it's his job to make sure the board operates effectively. Other board members come from both inside and outside of the company. Inside board members work for the corporation, often holding key posts in upper-level management. Outside board members don't work for the company, and their role is to offer independent and unbiased points of view.

The board's responsibilities include duties such as:

- Communicating directly with corporate executives
- Framing and tracking high level corporate strategies
- Making sure the corporation and its management operate with integrity
- Approving the overall corporate budget
- Hiring the corporation's upper management team

That management team is responsible for implementing the strategies dictated by the board, and it is their responsibility to run the company for maximum profitability. Key players of a management team include the CEO (chief executive officer), CFO (chief financial officer), and COO (chief operations officer).

Ticker Trivia

Corporations may have presidents and vice presidents as part of their upper management teams. Typically, the president is second in command to the CEO, often doing double-duty as the COO. Vice presidents hold responsibility for different sections of the company (like marketing and product development) and report back to the president/COO.

The CEO is the main man in charge of everything, and he reports directly to the board. In most corporations, the CEO also sits on the board. The CFO is in charge of corporate finances and reporting.

He prepares budgets and financial statements as required, and is responsible for the financial health of the company. The COO is the most hands-on job of the three, responsible for the operations of the company, including personnel, marketing, and sales. The CFO and the COO both report to the CEO.

THE CEO PAY SCALE

CEOs can get paid almost unimaginable amounts of money, thanks to lucrative multiyear contracts that companies use to lure them into the job. Though it seems crazy, CEO compensation is based on how they're expected to perform, rather than on how well they actually do their jobs. This seemingly bizarre norm exists because corporations want to attract the best candidates to fill their top management spots.

Tracking their true pay can be tricky, though, because it doesn't all come in the form of straight salary. Corporate executives often enjoy substantial perks, like company cars, corporate jets, and generous expense accounts in addition to their sizeable salaries.

Many CEOs start with base salaries topping $1 million. That pay is guaranteed regardless of the corporation's success or failure. With higher base salaries, the CEO may be less driven to work hard to improve the company's profitability and future prospects.

Next come bonuses, but these may not work the way shareholders expect. Guaranteed bonuses are really just ways of paying a higher salary without calling it that. Performance-based bonuses require the CEO to meet specific goals, and those bonuses are only paid out when the goals are achieved. As you'd expect, CEOs who get paid more if they perform well tend to work harder at maximizing shareholder value. Setting performance goals at that level, though, is not as simple as it appears. Though it might seem obvious to tie performance to revenues, profits, or share price, external forces can greatly affect any of those measures. A CEO might make tough choices that reduce profitability one year in order to set the stage for future growth, for example, or a competitor's misfortune could trigger a sales explosion that the CEO had no hand in.

One idea that's proven most effective is to connect CEO bonuses with shares of stock (rather than stock options, securities that allow their holder to buy shares of stock at a preset guaranteed price, which can encourage the executives to artificially influence stock prices for personal gain). This links what's best for the shareholders directly to the CEO's personal wealth.

How Much Did They Make?

You can find detailed information about a CEO's salary and bonuses on Form DEF 14A, which is part of the information that is required in the corporation's SEC filings. The company's proxy statement contains information on stock and stock option ownership by upper management, called "beneficial ownership."

A LOOK AT THE UNREAL NUMBERS

When you get a first glimpse at a CEO's salary, you may think your eyes are playing tricks on you. They're not. Top corporate executive pay continues to grow, and the chasm between their pay and the pay of the average American is truly mind-boggling.

Consider this: According to a 2014 report by the AFL-CIO (a group of labor organizations), the typical salary of a CEO working for a corporation listed on the S&P 500 was 373 times higher than the average worker. Executive salary tracking firm Equilar revealed that the median CEO compensation package for 2015 rang in at $17.6 million a year. That's the median CEO pay, and it pales in comparison to what the highest-paid executives earn. Some of the top CEO salaries for 2015 (according to Equilar) went to:

- $156.1 million: CEO David Zaslav, Discovery Communications
- $111.9 million: CEO Michael Fries, Liberty Global
- $88.5 million: CEO Mario Gabelli, GAMCO Investors
- $42.1 million: CEO Marissa Mayer, Yahoo!

Now consider this: David Zaslav's annual pay was 1,951 times higher than the median $80,000 employee salary at Discovery Communications, according to a study by Glassdoor (a jobs and recruiting website). Soon, the new SEC disclosure rule (which kicks in when corporate financial statements for 2017 are filed in 2018) will require corporations to publish the CEO pay ratio, comparing the top executive's compensation to that of the median company employee.

BAD CEOS

Many, if not most, CEOs act in the best interests of the corporations they work for. Sometimes, though, the CEO is so spectacularly greedy, selfish, or incompetent that he demolishes the company, leaving stunned stockholders with intolerable losses and substantially devalued shares.

Excessive pay is just one of the ways CEOs can loot their employers. People in this position can make more than $100,000 a day, even if they're doing a terrible job. Meanwhile, they also benefit from a combination of bonuses (which are not even necessarily based on performance) and perks, like luxury cars and trips on the corporate jet.

As if that's not enough, some CEOs take even further advantage of their positions, with no regard for the shareholders they're supposed to serve. For example, they can guarantee loans for themselves, or have the corporation buy assets from other companies they own or are associated with (like a brother-in-law's office furniture company). While these types of actions are clear conflicts of interest and technically illegal, they're rarely prosecuted because it's nearly impossible to prove the legal case. After all, that brother-in-law's office furniture could truly be the best deal in town.

Take the case of former Disney CEO Michael Eisner, whose tenure was marked by drama and upheaval. To make sure every decision went his way, Eisner (as chairman) stacked the board of directors with his own picks, and that group backed some very poor choices. In 2002, the Disney stock price fell to its lowest level in eight years. By 2004, the corporation's earnings didn't even come close to Wall Street projections, disappointing analysts and shareholders alike. And during that fateful time, Eisner managed to alienate Pixar Animation Studios, one of Disney's major holdings and most successful film partners. But none of that stopped Eisner from accepting an outrageous bonus of $7.25 million. Then, in March 2004, faced with a laundry list of failures, Eisner lost the confidence of the board, and was removed from his position as chairman of the board. Shortly after that, in March 2005, Eisner finally resigned, leaving Disney in the capable hands of current CEO Robert Iger.

SHAREHOLDERS TAKE A STAND

When a shareholder has a vested interest in a corporation's success but doesn't approve of the way the top brass is running the company, he can take action. In fact, shareholder activism can sometimes be very successful.

To really turn the tide and make an impact, a given shareholder needs a healthy stake of the company, usually around 10%. If that active shareholder happens to have a following or a lot of influence, other shareholders will join his crusade, and that's when things really start to heat up.

With enough support, a shareholder activist can sway the vote when it comes to electing board members. New and like-minded board members can put a lot of pressure on the top executives, strongly encouraging (if not outright forcing) them to clean up their acts.

Many of the changes shareholder activists favor involve frivolous, wasteful spending by upper management. Examples of excessive spending include things like a collection of corporate jets, first-class travel accommodations, entertainment expenses, extravagant parties, and hefty bonuses unrelated to performance.

After all, the shareholders own the company; it's their money that's being spent. Many invest for the long haul, and expect the corporate management to focus on long-term growth and gains rather than on season tickets and expensive "retreats" in Las Vegas. By actively asserting their collective force, shareholders can spark the kind of change that turns lackluster performance into solid profits.

One of the most famous active shareholders is Carl Icahn. Corporate executives break into a cold sweat when he sets his sights on them. Take his involvement in Time Warner, for example. After their ill-fated merger with AOL, the company's actions sent stock prices plummeting. In 2006, dismayed by the results of the clearly failing business combination, Icahn gathered up shareholder support and demanded that some changes be made and actions be taken. Among those demands: implement cost-cutting measures to increase profitability; make a $20 billion stock buyback by the corporation; and split the troubled mega-corporation into four separate companies. The activist group won two out of three, the buyback and the expense reductions (worth $1 billion). The group also put new members on the board of directors.

SOMETIMES CORPORATIONS FAIL

Investing in the stock market has ups and downs; share prices rise and fall. Sometimes, though, it's more than market sentiment that causes an investment to tank. Not every company is successful. And, as we learned the hard way back in 2008, even very big, reputable, and seemingly stable companies can crumble into nothing.

When a public company goes bankrupt, shareholders are inevitably hurt. The stock itself is worthless on the market, so the only way investors can recoup any money at all is if there's anything left over after all the creditors are paid. Whether shareholders get any money out of the liquidation (asset selloff) depends on several factors, including what type of stock they own.

When a public corporation goes bankrupt, it follows the same basic steps as any other company. First, the firm must sell all of its assets. With those proceeds, the company then pays off any and all debts, starting with money owed to the U.S. government (usually back taxes, interest, and penalties). Once creditors have been satisfied, the company must pay its bondholders; not all corporations issue bonds, so some skip this step. Next on the list are preferred stockholders, with common stockholders bringing up the rear.

Much of the time, common stockholders end up with nothing. However, if there is any money left after all other claims have been paid, the common stockholders will split the pot based on the percentage of shares they hold. For example, if the company has $150,000 left, a 1% shareholder would receive $1,500.

COMMON STOCK

The Powers of Ownership

Common stocks are basic equity securities that are sold to the public, and each share constitutes ownership in a corporation. When people talk about trading shares, they're talking about common stock.

Corporations come in all sizes. You can invest in a wildly successful mega-cap company or a micro-cap company that is just beginning to show signs of growth potential. Some people prefer to buy the common stock of well-established companies, while other investors would rather invest in smaller, growth-oriented companies.

No matter what type of company fits in with your overall investing strategy, it's important to research every stock you consider buying. Just because a company has been around for decades doesn't mean it's the best investment choice for you. On top of that, companies are always changing, and it's important to make sure that the information you're reviewing is the most current available.

One of the first things to review is a company's market capitalization, or the market value of all of the company's outstanding shares. To calculate the market capitalization, multiply the current market price of a stock by the number of outstanding shares. The number of outstanding shares refers to the number of shares that have been sold to the public.

In addition to market cap, there are also different categories of stocks, enough to round out any portfolio. The variety includes blue chip, growth, cyclical, defensive, value, income, and speculative stocks.

- Blue chips are prestigious, well-known companies.
- Growth stocks are companies poised to expand their sales and markets.

- Cyclicals are strongly tied to economic ups and downs.
- Defensive stocks protect your portfolio against market downturns.
- Value stocks offer more worth than their prices imply.
- Income stocks pay steady dividends.
- Speculative stocks have the potential to skyrocket or crash.

PREFERRED STOCK

First in Line for Everything

Like common shares, preferred stock represents a piece of ownership in a company—but that's where the resemblance ends. As the name suggests, preferred stockholders receive preferential treatment in two very important ways: They have first dibs on dividends, and they are at the head of the line for going-out-of-business payouts, should the corporation face bankruptcy and liquidation.

Fixed Income

Preferred stock is usually considered a fixed-income investment, even though it's technically an equity investment. That's because preferred stock shares typically come with fixed, guaranteed dividend payments, a form of steady income. In fact, preferred stock is sometimes referred to as "the stock that acts like a bond."

Preferred stocks are hybrid securities that have almost as much in common with bonds as they do with common stock. Essentially, this type of stock comes with a redemption date and a promised dividend that gets paid regardless of the company's earnings. Also like bonds, some preferred stock can be callable, which means that the corporation has the right to buy back those shares at any time, usually for a premium over their market value. If the corporation has financial difficulties, holders of preferred stock have "seniority" and priority when it comes to dividend payments, and usually rate higher dividends than common shares.

There are some drawbacks to owning preferred stock, though. As the owner of preferred stock, you normally don't have the rights that come with common stock ownership, like voting. In addition, when a company's common stock price experiences strong growth, preferred prices tend to hold steady. Finally, when a corporation has a phenomenal year and pays out giant dividends on its common shares, preferred share dividend payments are usually locked in, and those shareholders don't get to share in the company's windfall.

How to Buy Preferred Stock

For investors, buying (or selling) preferred stock works the same way as trading common stock. All it takes is a call to a broker to add these hybrid securities to a portfolio.

For income-oriented investors, however, preferred stock can make a good portfolio addition. And though they aren't as prevalent as common stock, many corporations offer preferred shares. These companies include Allstate, Wells Fargo, Capital One, and T-Mobile.

PREFERRED DIVIDENDS

When it comes to receiving dividends, preferred shareholders have priority—they get paid first. Normally, this kind of stock comes with a fixed dividend, paid out every quarter. The dividend payout is calculated based on the par value of the stock, which never changes, so shareholders always know exactly how much they're getting.

For example, if ABC Corporation issues 5 million shares of 5% preferred stock with a par value of $30 per share, every quarter they would pay out a total of $1,875,000 in dividends (5% × $30 per share × 5,000,000 shares = $7,500,000 (per year) ÷ four = $1,875,000 per quarter).

PARTICIPATING PREFERRED STOCK

In times of prosperity, common shareholders can enjoy a fatter slice of the corporate earnings in the form of bigger dividend checks, while standard preferred stockholders receive their standard percentage. This drawback to preferred shares can be overcome with a special form of the security known as participating preferred.

Participating Poison

Corporations don't often issue participating preferred stock anymore, unless it's to be used as a defensive strategy. To help prevent a hostile takeover, a company may issue this type of stock along with the right to buy up new shares of common stock at bargain basement prices if an unwanted takeover begins. Here, the participating preferred shares act like a poison pill defense.

Participating preferred shareholders get two slices of the pie: First, they get their standard fixed percent of par dividend as promised, plus they may get a second dividend payout that is based on current corporate earnings. Typically, this double dip only comes around if the common shareholders enjoy an extraordinarily high dividend, specifically a dividend that's higher than the one the pre-ferred shareholders are slated to get.

For example, let's say ABC Corporation offers participating pre-ferred stock with a fixed dividend of $1.50 per share, and a second dividend payment that's activated any time the common stock divi-dends exceeds that. After a banner quarter, the ABC Corp. board of directors declares a $2.00 per share common stock dividend. The participating preferred shareholders would receive a total of $2.00 per share in dividends: their original $1.50 dividend plus a participa-tion dividend of fifty cents per share.

CUMULATIVE PREFERRED STOCK

Sometimes, corporations simply don't have enough cash on hand to pay out dividends, even to preferred shareholders whose dividend payments are supposed to be guaranteed. This can happen when times are tough, and a company is barely treading water and needs every penny to keep itself afloat.

In these down times, when a corporation must suspend dividend payments in order to pay their bills (and their employees), preferred stockholders are left in the lurch. Unless, that is, they have cumula-tive preferred shares.

Cumulative preferred shares come with what's basically a "catch-up" provision. When the company once again has ample cash on hand, these preferred shareholders are entitled to receive all of the previously skipped dividends before the common stockholders can get any dividends at all.

CONVERTIBLES

The Sofa Beds of the Stock Market

For investors who want to minimize the rollercoaster ride built into owning stocks but still want to have a toe in the stock market, convertible securities offer the best of both worlds, even though they do carry some risk. Convertibles can refer to either bonds or preferred stock shares, but here we'll primarily focus on convertible preferred stock.

Convertible preferred stock starts out just like regular preferred stock: It acts like a cross between common stock and a bond. These fixed income securities provide a steady supply of income through ongoing dividend payments. But convertible shares have an extra feature not available on standard preferred stock: Holders can trade them in for a specific number of shares (called the conversion ratio) of common stock with full voting and participation rights.

Convertible preferred shares trade on the open market, and pricing is based on a conversion premium. How convertible shares trade depends on what's going on with the common stock price. When the market price is higher than the conversion price, the shares sell like stock. But when the market price dips below the conversion price, the convertible preferred shares trade like bonds, for a premium. The conversion ratio helps investors figure out when it makes sense to trade in their preferred shares for common shares. To benefit from conversion, the common stock must be trading for more than the conversion price, which is calculated by dividing the preferred share price by the conversion ratio.

For example, say you bought 100 shares of ABC Corp. preferred stock for $50 per share. The stock has a conversion ration of five to one: Every share of preferred stock you own can be traded in for five shares of common stock. The conversion price here would be $10 per share, which is the $50 preferred share price divided by the conversion ratio of 5. If the common shares were trading for more than $10 per share, it would pay to convert. But if they were trading for less than $10 per share, you would lose money on the conversion. For example, if ABC common shares were selling for $8 per share, a conversion would bring you $40 ($8 × 5 shares), which is less than the $50 you paid for the ABC preferred share.

CAPS: Convertible Adjustable Preferred Stock

A corporation may offer CAPS, which are preferred shares that come with floating dividend payments that reset periodically. These shares come with the potential to convert into common stock like regular convertible preferred shares plus the promise that their dividend payments will remain competitive.

STOCK CLASSES

My Stock's Better Than Your Stock

Not all shares of stock are created equal. Aside from the fundamental difference between common and preferred stocks, corporations can issue customized classes of stock with special features in pretty much any way they want. The main reason a corporation would do this is to concentrate power in a particular group of shareholders, which is why the most common class distinction has to do with voting rights.

Common shares issued with extra voting rights are known as super voting shares, and their purpose is to keep corporate insiders, such as the founders and key management personnel, in charge. Most often, super voting shares come with ten votes per share, as opposed to the standard one-vote-one-share power of regular common stock. However, there's no rule limiting the number of allowable votes per share, so corporations can set them much higher than ten to one.

Getting More Common

Back in 2005, about 1% of initial public offerings (IPOs) included more than one class of common stock. That number leaped up to 12% in 2014, and hit 15.5% in 2015.

Super shares are usually designated as Class A, with regular shares labeled Class B. That's the standard, but not all corporations follow that convention. You would be wise to double check if a prospective company offers stock in multiple classes. Google, for example, when it first incorporated issued Class B shares that carried ten votes apiece for its founders and chief executives. It also issued Class A shares for the general investing public, who get one vote per share. Both classes of shares can be listed and traded on the major exchanges.

While they do have more voting power, super shares usually don't own a bigger portion of the company or its earnings than standard shares do; these facets of stock ownership remain in one-to-one proportion as regular shares.

Examples of companies that use a dual-class stock structure include Fitbit and Facebook.

A CLASSIC CLASS EXAMPLE

One of the most famous cases of a corporation with different stock classes is Berkshire Hathaway (BRK), Warren Buffett's flagship company. Berkshire Hathaway has two classes of shares, Class A and Class B, and they're as different as night and ping pong balls.

Ticker Trivia

Berkshire Hathaway Class B shares, also known as Baby Bs, provide a special tax benefit for Berkshire Hathaway investors: These shares can be given as gifts to heirs without triggering any gift tax as Class A shares would.

The first glaring difference between the two share classes is price: Class A (traded as BRK.A) is priced at $214,000 per share (as of May 2016), the most expensive stock in the world; Class B (traded as BRK.B) trades at $142.60. The price of the Class A shares remains exorbitantly high because Buffett has vowed to never split the stock. He does this to attract "like-minded" investors who plan to buy the stock and hold on to it, and thus garner long-term appreciation and profits. Class A shares also come with 200-times-stronger voting rights, and the shares can be converted into Class B shares at the whim of the investor.

Class B was created back in 1996 to offer more flexibility to Berkshire Hathaway's shareholders and to allow smaller investors a chance to participate in the corporation's celebrated success. The initial 517,000 shares were launched at a price of $1,180 per share, one-thirtieth of the price of a single Class A share, at that time hovering around $34,000. In 2010, the Class B shares underwent a fifty-to-one stock split, bringing the price down from $3,476 per share to around $70 per share, keeping the stock affordable for small investors.

BLUE CHIPS

Silver Spoon Stocks

Of the thousands of stocks traded every day, only a few hundred are considered valuable enough to be called blue chips. Blue chips are considered to be the most prestigious, well-established companies that are publicly traded. Many of them have practically become household names. Included in this mostly large-cap mix are Walt Disney (DIS), McDonald's (MCD), ExxonMobil (XOM), and Wal-Mart (WMT). A good number of blue chip companies have been in existence for decades and still lead the pack in their respective industries. Since most of these corporations have solid track records, they are good investment vehicles for individuals who lean to the conservative side in their stock picks.

Literally Blue Chips

Back in the early 1920s, Dow Jones employee Oliver Gingold coined the phrase "blue chips" when talking about high value corporations. He named them after the blue chips used in poker games, the highest value chips on the table.

Let's take a look at how a portfolio can benefit from holding a blue chip stock. If you had purchased 100 shares of Wal-Mart stock on January 31, 1990, you would have paid around $4,200. Within the next five years, Wal-Mart called for two 2-for-1 stock splits, meaning you would now hold 400 shares. By January 31, 1995, your shares would have been worth $18,400—more than quadrupling your

Top: Alexander Hamilton (1755–1804), as seen on the face of the $10 bill. George Washington installed Alexander Hamilton as the first Secretary of the Treasury in 1789. Under his watch, the U.S. stock market was born.

Bottom: The exterior of the New York Stock Exchange at 11 Wall Street in lower Manhattan. Owned by Intercontinental Exchange, the building was designated a National Historic Landmark in 1978.

The trading floor of the New York Stock Exchange.

Contrary to strong, "bullish" times in the economy, a bear market is when the economy is on a downturn. Whether the market is characterized as bull o bear depends mainly on the prevailing direction of stock prices.

The most notorious black market day occurred in 1929: Black Tuesday. On Tuesday, October 29, 1929, the U.S. stock market tanked, setting off the Great Depression. The Depression lasted ten years, and remains the longest-lasting economic downturn in the history of the Western world. Today, this dark time in American history is memorialized in images such as George Segal's *Depression Breadline* sculpture, which can be found in Washington, D.C., at the Franklin Delano Roosevelt Memorial—a tribute to the president whose policies helped move the country out of the Depression.

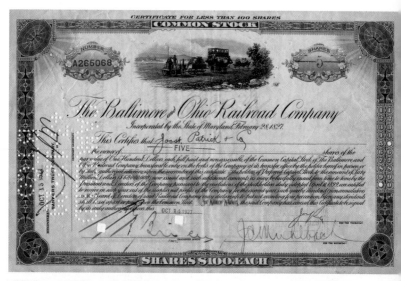

Stock certificates evolved over the years, as evident in these relics from the 18th and 20th centuries. The United States, among other countries, has embraced electronic registration. Public and private companies are no longer required to issue paper certificates to stockholders.

EURUSD 1.4923 1.49

USDJPY 89.39 89.42

USDCHF 1.0111 1.0115

GBPUSD 1.6779 1.6782

GBPJPY 150.00 150.07

EURCHF 1.5090 1.5095

etween the 1870s and 1970s, stock performance was communicated through ticker tape—
per strips that ran through stock ticker machines, which printed abbreviated company names as
ell as stock prices. The scrolling electronic tickers we see today maintain the same concept.

The exterior of J.P. Morgan, the largest bank in the United States. The man himself (1837–1913) was one of the most famous tycoons ever to trade on Wall Street. Morgan invested in dozens of enterprises, from railroads to steel mills to Thomas Edison's electric company. Despite tangles with antitrust laws, Congressional investigations, and his reputation as a callous robber baron, Morgan twice bailed out the U.S. government during financial panics. In fact, during the Panic of 1907, Morgan pledged his money (and convinced others to join him) to stabilize the U.S. banking system.

Portrait of Cornelius Vand[...]
(1794–1877). Born into pov[...]
Vanderbilt later would come [...]
the markets with a vengeance[...]
ruthlessly taking over companie[...]
and industries while employing
strategies never before seen.
Vanderbilt became a self-made
millionaire, leaving an estate worth
an estimated $105 million.

Image produced by Mathew Brady's studio; restored
by Michel Vuijlsteke

Known as the richest man in
the world, John D. Rockefeller
(1839–1937) was notorious for
his cutthroat business strategies,
which included crushing his
competition, then buying up all
their assets.

Image Source: The Rockefeller Archive Center

Andrew Carnegie (1835–1919) as he appears in the National Portrait Gallery. He famously led the expansion of the American steel industry in the late 1800s, earning hundreds of millions of dollars in the process. One key secret to Carnegie's vast financial success was an idea called vertical combination: He bought majority shares in the iron mines necessary to steel manufacturing, as well as shares in the railroads to move his products increasing overall efficiency and reducing costs for the core business. He was also a note philanthropist, giving more than $350 million to charity during his lifetime, including the funding to build Carnegie Hall in New York City.

Photograph by Billy Hathorn (original artist unknown)

original investment. And by January 31, 2008, after yet another 2-for-1 split which brought your holdings up to 800 shares, your investment would have been worth $40,000, almost ten times more than your original purchase price. Though Wal-Mart shares last split in 1999, the company's stock price has stayed strong. By January 31, 2016, your investment would have been worth $52,800, and that doesn't even include dividends received over the years!

Most blue chip companies have market capitalization in the billions, but that's not the only criteria for inclusion into this exclusive group. What other factors land corporations in this subjective category? A solid track record of weathering economic turbulence, a creditworthy reputation, healthy financial fitness, reliable earnings, consistent growth, and steady dividends.

VALUE STOCKS

Get More for Less

Value stocks appear inexpensive when compared to their corporate earnings, dividends, sales, or other fundamental factors. Basically, you're getting more than what you pay for, which makes it a good value. When investors are high on growth stocks, value stocks tend to be ignored, making them even better bargains for savvy investors. Value investors believe that these stocks make the best buys given their reasonable price in relation to many growth stocks. Of course, a good value is highly dependent on current stock prices, so a good value today might not be a good value next month. A good rule of thumb is to look for solid companies that are trading at no more than three times their book value per share. An example of good value (at least as of July 2016) is AT&T, with a price-to-book value ratio of 2.10.

VALUE INVESTING

Value investors are on the prowl for bargains, and they're more inclined than growth investors to analyze companies by using such data as sales volume, earnings, and cash flow. The philosophy here is that value companies are actually undervalued, so their stock price doesn't truly represent how much they're worth. In fact, value investors often ignore share prices because they have nothing to do with the company's worth. Rather, the value to these investors is in the potential returns that come with buying and holding a good business.

Value investors are often willing to ride out stock price fluctuations because of the extensive research they have done prior to committing to a particular stock. Often, value stocks are found in established industries that are no longer in vogue but have proven track records coupled with low growth expectations. Keep in mind that low growth doesn't mean *no* growth—it just means growth rates that are lower than companies in emerging or popular industries. In times of economic uncertainty, though, value stocks may hold their own while other types of stocks falter.

Ticker Trivia

Famed financial guru Benjamin Graham pioneered the value investing style, focusing attention on what companies were actually worth rather than on share price movement.

You can identify value stocks by their relatively low price ratios (which include the price-to-earnings ratio (P/E ratio), price-to-sales ratio, and price-to-book value ratio), lower-than-average growth rates, and PEG (price-to-earnings growth) less than 1, which means that the company's growth potential isn't yet reflected in its price. Examples of value stocks (at the time of this writing) include American Express (AXP), AT&T (T), and Tyson Foods (TSN). Keep in mind that once these stocks catch fire they may lose their value status as demand drives prices up.

INCOME STOCKS

Keep Sending Those Dividend Checks

Income stocks do just what their name suggests: provide steady income streams for investors. These shares come with regular dividends, sometimes big enough that people can actually live off their dividend payments. Though many income stocks fall into the blue chip category, other types of stocks (like value stocks) may offer consistent dividend payments as well. These stocks make a good addition to fixed-income portfolios, as they also provide the opportunity for share-price growth.

Income stocks may fit the bill if generating income is your primary goal. One example of an income stock is public utility companies; such stocks have traditionally paid higher dividends than other types of stock. In addition, preferred stocks make excellent income vehicles, typically providing steady dividends and high yields. As with some other types of stock, it's wise to look for a solid company with a good track record, especially when you're counting on a strong reliable income stream.

Examples of strong income stocks include:

- Staples (SPLS) with 5.51% dividends
- Target (TGT) with 3.25% dividends
- Best Buy (BBY) with 3.50% dividends
- Mattel (MAT) with 4.78% dividends
- Barnes & Noble (BKS) with 5.17% dividends
- General Motors (GM) with 4.84% dividends

GROWTH STOCKS

Buy Low, Sell High

Growth stocks, as you can probably guess from the name, include companies that have strong growth potential. Many companies in this category have sales, earnings, and market share that are growing faster than the overall economy. Such stocks usually represent companies that are big on research and development. Pioneers in new technologies are often growth-stock companies. Earnings in these companies are usually put right back into the business, rather than paid out to shareholders as dividends.

Growth stocks may be riskier than their blue chip counterparts, but in many cases you may also reap greater rewards. Generally speaking, growth stocks perform best during bull markets, while value stocks perform best during bear markets. Of course that's not guaranteed. A word of caution: beware of stocks whose price seems to be growing faster than would make sense. Sometimes momentum traders will help run growth-stock prices to sky-scraping levels then sell them off, causing the stock price to plummet.

GROWTH INVESTING

Essentially, growth investors want to own a piece of the fastest-growing companies around, even if it means paying a hefty price for this privilege. Growth companies are organizations that have experienced rapid growth, such as Microsoft. They may have outstanding management teams, highly rated developments, or plans for aggressive expansion into foreign markets. Growth-company stocks rarely pay significant dividends, and growth investors don't expect them to. Instead, growth companies plow their earnings right back into the business to promote even more growth. Among other things, growth investors pay close attention to company earnings. If growth investing fits in with their overall strategy, investors would do well to look for companies that have demonstrated strong growth over the past several years.

NIFTY 50

The "Nifty 50" comprises a group of corporations poised for significant growth. Institutional investors identified the companies in the original group in the running bull markets of the 1960s and 1970s. To make the list, these predominantly large-cap companies had to have strong prospects, and most had high price-to-earnings ratios (P/E ratios) and demonstrated steady earnings growth.

Ticker Trivia

Nifty 50 stocks were sometimes called "one-decision" stocks, because investors would buy them for the long haul with no intent to sell them.

Of that initial set, which included companies like Coca-Cola and IBM, very few count as growth companies today. Many of the first Nifty 50 companies no longer exist, such as Polaroid, and several others, like Xerox, are experiencing financial troubles. This alone serves as evidence that the market, and even the most solid companies, can change dramatically, reminding investors not to hang their hats on any company before doing detailed research.

In 2008, a new Nifty 50 list was created by financial titan UBS. The new picks include about a quarter of the original list along with some modern global giants:

- Coca-Cola (KO)
- Microsoft (MSFT)
- Philip Morris International (PM)
- Walt Disney (DIS)
- Bristol-Myers Squibb (BMY)

CYCLICAL STOCKS

Lather, Rinse, Repeat

Companies with earnings that are strongly tied to the economic cycle are considered to be cyclical. Economic cycles can last for months or years, but they always follow the same pattern, and they are greatly affected by the economy as a whole. When the economy picks up momentum, cyclical stocks follow this positive trend. When the economy slows down, these stocks slow down, too.

Cyclical industries include car manufacturers, hotels, and airlines—things that could be considered luxuries rather than necessities. When the economy is flying high, people buy more cars and take more vacations, and these cyclical industries benefit, and cyclical stock prices rise. But when the economy slows down, and people tighten their belts, these cyclical industries typically see a huge drop in sales and earnings, and so cyclical stock prices drop.

Making money with cyclical stocks can be very tricky, and is wholly dependent on getting in and out at just the right time. To do that, you must be well-versed in the ups and downs of business cycles and in tune with the economy, or you could end up losing your shirt.

Cyclical stocks would include companies like General Motors (GM), Royal Caribbean Cruises (RCL), and Hilton Worldwide Holdings (HLT).

DEFENSIVE STOCKS

These Linebackers Protect Your Portfolio

Defensive stocks offer stable earnings and steady dividends under most economic conditions, no matter what is going on in the rest of the market. During down or uncertain times, defensive stocks are the ones to own. They are considered noncyclical, meaning they don't follow the standard economic cycles like other stocks can. For that reason they often perform better than other stocks during down cycles. However, even when the rest of the stock market is climbing high, these solid shares tend to keep that same steady pace.

That's mainly because these companies sell products we all need all the time, and can't live without. Stocks that fall into this category include food companies, clothing companies, and utility companies. These businesses cover the basic necessities of life: food, clothing, and shelter.

Not every business that falls into one of those categories, though, would be considered defensive. Companies like General Mills, and other brands you can find in the grocery store, count as defensive stocks in the food category. Restaurant stocks, on the other hand, typically don't.

Companies considered to be defensive stocks in their respective categories can change, though that seems counterintuitive. Consider utilities: You can't run your house without electricity, heat, or water. But these days, the telephone utility, what we now call "home phones," isn't a necessity for everyone. This means that the old style telephone companies are no longer defensive stocks in the utilities category. Similarly, as companies like Netflix continue to draw customers, traditional cable companies will likely fall out of the defensive stock category as well.

Ticker Trivia

Don't confuse defensive stocks with defense stocks. Defense stocks refer specifically to companies that manufacture and supply items such as guns, ammunition, tanks, submarines, and missiles.

The list of defensive stocks includes titans such as General Mills (GIS), Johnson & Johnson (JNJ), and ConAgra Foods (CAG).

TECH STOCKS

Tomorrow's Trends or Yesterday's News

Technology companies cover a very broad range, from physical products like computers, semiconductors (chips), and smartphones to video game software, online retailers, and biotech (a marriage of biology and technology). They provide products and services to individuals and businesses, and constantly improve, upgrade, and create things that were once considered science fiction. Any of these types of businesses that are publicly traded count as tech stocks.

Some of the most well-known and largest technology companies include:

- Amazon.com (AMZN)
- eBay (EBAY)
- Netflix (NFLX)
- Apple (AAPL)
- Facebook (FB)

Tech stocks typically trade for more than the corporations are worth on paper, with a lot of value placed on their expected future innovations and success. With limited cash and capital assets standard for the category, these companies trade on ideas and development. Sometimes that pays off, other times they miss the mark and the companies just disappear.

PENNY STOCKS

You Get What You Pay For

Penny stocks are stocks that sell for $5 or less, and in many cases you're lucky if they're worth even that much. Most penny stocks usually have no substantial income or revenue. You have a high potential for loss with penny stocks. If you have a strong urge to invest in this type of company, take time out to follow the stock to see if it has made any headway. Learn all you can about the company, and don't be tempted to act on a hot tip that may have been passed your way.

The companies behind these stocks are thinly capitalized and are often not required to file reports with the SEC. They trade over the counter, and there is a limited amount of public information available. This in itself is reason for concern. How many astute investors want to put their money into an investment offering little or no information? Nonetheless, people do invest in these stocks.

One of the most interesting—and alarming—aspects of penny stock dealing is that brokers are not always acting as a third party but instead set prices and act as the principals in the transaction. Penny stocks most often do not have a single price but a number of different prices at which they can be purchased or sold.

Okay, so there's little information about the company, the price, or anything else to investigate. But the guy on the phone—making a cold call—says it will be the next Starbucks! This is where they get you. Thanks to the Internet and the selling of phone lists, penny stocks dealers can reach out far and wide. They use high-pressure sales tactics and armies of callers, and they will tell you anything to make you buy the stocks. Beware!

All of this is not to say that there are no low-priced legitimate stocks on the market. There are. They are usually small grassroots companies that can grow over time—if you pick the right one and wait a while. You should invest cautiously and conservatively at first. Look for a new company with good leadership in an industry where you see growth potential. It's also advantageous to find a company that holds the patent on a new product. If the product takes off, so could your stock. You must actively seek out all of this information— it will not come to you via a cold caller.

DIVIDENDS

Money for Nothing

When a corporation is operating profitably and ends a fiscal period with plenty of cash on hand, its directors need to decide what to do with that money. They could choose to reinvest the surplus cash in the business, hoping to spur further profits. They could decide to pay down the corporate debt, or buy up another company. In many cases, though, successful corporations opt to share their windfalls with their shareholders. When they do distribute that extra cash to their investors, they are paying out dividends.

Dividends are payments made to shareholders that have nothing to do with stock price. These payouts are made simply because the company has reaped healthy profits and chooses to reward its shareholders. The corporate board of directors will decide whether and how often to pay a dividend to shareholders based on just how profitable the company is and how much cash they have on hand.

Dividends are usually more important to investors looking for income, and stocks that regularly pay dividends are thus known as income stocks. Many established companies pay dividends on a quarterly basis, and special one-time dividends may also be paid under certain circumstances.

When a company decides to pay dividends, the payout is based on its shares outstanding. The term "shares outstanding" refers to the number of shares a company has issued to the general public, including its employees. More shares outstanding can mean smaller dividends per shareholder; there's only so much money to go around, after all.

TRACKING DIVIDENDS

Before buying a stock for the dividends it's paying today, take a look at the dividends it's paid in the past. Compare the current dividend with the dividends paid over the past five years. Shrinking dividends may indicate plans for expansion; when a company's primary goal is growth, dividends may be small or nonexistent. To decide if a specific dividend stock makes sense for your portfolio, it's a good idea to compare it to other dividend stocks using the dividend yields.

The dividend yield converts the dollar value of an annual dividend (whether it's paid in cash or shares) into a percentage, allowing you to see the return rate. To compute the dividend yield, divide the annual dividend per share by the stock's share price. For example, if a corporation pays out a dividend of $0.50 per share, and the stock is trading at $25 per share, the dividend yield would equal 2% (0.50 ÷ 25 = 0.02).

DIVIDEND DATES

When it comes to reaping the benefits of a successful corporate year, shareholders need to pay attention to four very important dates:

1. Declaration date
2. Ex-dividend date
3. Date of record
4. Payable date

Corporations set these dates to make sure the right person receives the dividend check, and with stocks trading constantly, that can be a daunting task. So if you are buying or selling a stock that comes with a dividend payout, make sure you know your dates.

The declaration date is the day the corporate board of directors announces that a dividend will be paid. This typically comes in the form of a public announcement, such as a press release, and possibly direct notification to shareholders (which now is typically done by e-mail).

The ex-dividend date (sometimes also called the ex-date) is very important for people trading a stock for which a dividend has been declared. On and after the ex-dividend date, the stock trades without the dividend; if you buy a stock during this period, you will not receive the declared dividend. The ex-dividend date falls two days before the day of record.

Ticker Trivia

The ex-dividend date is necessary because there's a time lag between the day you buy a stock and the day the corporation records you as a shareholder.

The date of record is the day on which the corporation figures out exactly who gets the dividend checks. Only the shareholder of record on that day will receive the dividend payout.

As you might expect, the payable date refers to the day the dividend checks are mailed to the shareholders of record. This date often falls about a week after the date of record.

STOCK DIVIDENDS

Sometimes, instead of paying out dividends in cash, a corporation will reward its stockholders by issuing shares of stock as dividends.

This can happen when a corporation has positive earnings, but is short on cash or wants to use its cash reserves for another purpose.

Stock dividends are paid out of a corporation's treasury stock, which refers to shares of its own stock that the corporation holds. If the corporation doesn't have any treasury stock, it cannot pay out a stock dividend.

Here's how it works. Let's say QXZ Corporation had a stellar year and wants to pay dividends to its shareholders. There isn't enough cash stockpiled to pay everyone, but QXZ has treasury stock on hand. So QXZ opts to issue 0.05 dividend shares for each share a stockholder owns. If you owned 500 shares of QXZ, you would receive twenty-five new shares as your dividend.

If you happened to end up with any fractional shares, those would normally be paid out as cash. For example, if you owned 525 shares of QXZ, and the company declared a 0.05 stock dividend, your stock dividend would be 26.25 shares. Since you cannot trade a quarter of a share, you would get cash instead.

DRIPS

For investors who like the idea of earning dividends but don't need the cash, dividend reinvestment plans, known as DRIPs, will help their investments grow more quickly. Many companies that pay regular dividends offer these plans so that stockholders can automatically reinvest their dividends in extra shares.

Dividend reinvestment plans offer shareholders a simple and inexpensive way to purchase stock directly through a company, without having to pay commissions. This type of investment plan does not require the services of a broker. Such plans enable investors to purchase small amounts of common stock right from the corporation itself—in many cases, as little as $25 worth of stock at a time. Depending on the company, there may be a small fee for handling your account. In most cases, you will have to already own at least one share of the stock (purchased through a broker) to be eligible to participate in the DRIP. And, as the name implies, this plan only works for stocks that pay regular dividends, which must be reinvested in the stock.

Consider this: If you received cash dividends but really wanted more shares in the company, you would take that cash and buy more stock. A DRIP does that for you, effortlessly. Every dollar of dividend you'd be entitled to is transformed into more shares, every time they pay out dividends.

To find out whether a company offers a DRIP, look at the investor relations section on the corporate website.

Keep in mind that, as with all dividend earnings, there will be a tax bill at the end of the year. Even though you don't actually receive any money (since your dividends are used to get you more stock), you will have to pay taxes on any dividends you earned. Along those lines, it's critical that you keep very good records of your DRIP account. When the time comes for you to sell shares, you'll need to know exactly how much money you've paid for them, including your reinvested dividends. That way you will be able to accurately calculate the capital gain (or loss) at the time of the sale.

STOCK SPLITS

Two Are Better Than One

A stock split works in virtually the same way as breaking a $20, changing that one $20 bill for two $10 bills. You'd still have the same amount of money, $20, but now you would have two bills instead of one. The mechanics of a stock split work just like that. In a two-for-one stock split, for example, each shareholder would get two shares for each single share he held before, and the price of each share would be split in half. The corporation increases the total number of its shares on the market without changing its total market capitalization.

Wal-Mart Splits

Since it was first issued in 1972, Wal-Mart stock has undergone eleven two-for-one stock splits.

Let's look at some numbers:

Suppose Spenser Corporation has 20 million shares outstanding, and the current share price is $30 per share, for a total market capitalization of $600 million (20 million shares × $30 per share). Spenser Corp. decides to execute a two-for-one stock split. Now there will be 40 million shares outstanding, and the per-share price will drop to $15. The total market capitalization hasn't changed at all: 40 million shares at $15 each still equals $600 million.

So if the market capitalization has not changed at all, why would a corporation bother to enact a stock split?

REASONS FOR STOCK SPLITS

There are two main reasons a corporation would split its stock: to lower the share price or to increase the liquidity.

The most common reason for a stock split relates directly to the stock price. When a share price gets too high, fewer people can afford to invest in it, especially in standard 100-share lots. For example, if a stock was trading at $50 per share, you would need $5,000 to buy 100 shares. But if the stock split two-for-one, bringing the share price down to $25, you would only need $2,500 to buy 100 shares. That price drop opens up the stock to many more potential investors.

Share liquidity is another reason corporations decide to implement stock splits, though this is less common. More shares on the market can bring more investors to the stock, making trading easier. This boost to share liquidity can push the bid-ask spread down, which also benefits investors.

DIFFERENT WAYS TO SPLIT

Not all stock splits use that two-for-one ratio. Other very common splits are three-for-one and three-for-two. And while none of those ratios affect the total market capitalization, each affects the shareholder and the share price differently.

Continuing the previous example, let's say Spenser Corp. called for a three-for-one split. Now there would be 60 million shares outstanding (three times the original 20 million shares), and the price per share would drop to $10.

REVERSE STOCK SPLITS

Just as the name implies, a reverse stock split is the opposite of a regular stock split. In a reverse stock split, a corporation reduces its total number of shares outstanding. This action is also sometimes called a share rollback or a stock consolidation.

Typically, corporations that engage in a reverse split divide their shares by five or ten: a one-for-five split or a one-for-ten split. In a one-for-ten split, for example, each shareholder would walk away with only one share for every ten shares he held before. However, that single share would now have a share price ten times higher than before.

Let's look at reverse split math. Suppose Brady Corporation had 10 million shares outstanding and was trading at $1 per share for a total market capitalization of $10 million. If Brady Corp. decided to initiate a one-for-ten reverse stock split, the original 10 million outstanding shares would shrink to 1 million shares, and the original $1 per share price would increase to $10 per share. And, just like with a traditional stock split, the market capitalization would remain unchanged.

Virtually all reverse stock splits come about because share prices have dropped too low for the corporation to maintain its exchange listing status. Under normal economic conditions, the major exchanges enforce a minimum share price of $4 for new listings, and $1 for companies that are already trading. Those rules have been suspended in times of deep economic trouble, like a sustained bear market.

MERGERS AND ACQUISITIONS

Let's Get Together

For hundreds of years, companies have come together through mergers and acquisitions. They do this primarily to increase shareholder value: Combining forces can provide a competitive edge, increasing the value of the resultant corporation for stockholders.

When two companies combine, whether through merger or acquisition, they can gain many potential advantages, such as better market share, reduced financial risk, cost savings, and increased profitability.

On the other hand, mixing two companies can also result in friction and conflict. Disparate corporate cultures can make it difficult for employees to work together efficiently. Integrating different computer systems, corporate processes, and business plans can lead to major sticking points as the new company goes through growing pains. In the worst cases, the new company cannot function effectively, and shareholders suffer as the stock price falls.

MERGERS

Mergers are deals where two companies come together as one, blending their businesses by mutual agreement of their boards of directors and with shareholder approval. Most commonly, when this happens a new combined company is formed. Shareholders of each original company would now own shares in the newly formed company.

There are three basic types of mergers:

1. Horizontal merger
2. Vertical merger
3. Circular merger

A horizontal merger involves the blending of two companies in the same industry. Before they combined, the two companies were competitors, selling the same products to the same customers. After they join forces, they consolidate their businesses into one stronger, more competitive corporation. The new larger company can be more profitable due to improved economies of scale. That means they can lower costs based on increased volume, similar to buying in bulk at the grocery store. DaimlerChrysler, the blending of Daimler-Benz and Chrysler, is an example of a horizontal merger.

In a vertical merger, two corporations that operate in different parts of the same business come together. Typically, each contributes different services or physical goods toward the same end product, like a soda manufacturer and a sugar producer both play a role in bringing soft drinks to the grocery store. The basic idea behind a vertical merger is to bring together companies that can operate more effectively as one company. With sugar now in-house, the soda manufacturer can reduce the cost to make their soft drinks, and even possibly grow the business by supplying sugar to other food and beverage producers.

Circular mergers diverge widely from the other merger types. These combinations strive to bring a broader range of products and services to their customers, sometimes mixing quite disparate companies. These can be the most risky types of mergers, especially if the companies joining forces don't really understand the business of the other. A circular merger could combine, for example, a makeup manufacturer with a soap and shampoo manufacturer.

Most mergers result in somewhat more successful corporations. Sometimes, though, the combination of two companies brings spectacular success, like Disney Pixar, where the market can hardly remember the separate companies that came before; other times, mergers can result in dismal failures.

EXXONMOBIL, A SUCCESSFUL MERGER

One of the most fruitful mergers in financial history happened back in 1999. Consistently low oil prices were plaguing the industry, and big oil corporations were looking for ways to turn the tide back toward exceptional profitability.

In this climate, Exxon and Mobil, two oil giants, agreed to merge. The deal went through for $81 billion, an amount critics and naysayers deemed too much, and Exxon Mobil Corporation was formed; at the time it was the largest corporation in the world. The combined forces of Exxon Mobil Corporation (XOM) thrived, and now the deal is considered one of the most successful mergers to ever grace the financial pages.

Together Again

The ExxonMobil merger had a noteworthy side effect. The deal reunited two previously separated companies: Standard Oil Company of New Jersey, which had come to be known as Exxon, and Standard Oil Company of New York, which was then called Mobil.

IMPACT ON SHAREHOLDERS

When two corporations plan to merge, both of their share prices begin to change unpredictably, causing a great deal of shareholder anxiety. Right before the deal is complete, share prices may spike or dip. Once that rollercoaster ride comes to an end, shareholders of both original companies can expect shares in the newly formed company to be higher.

In addition to price changes, shareholders can expect some differences in their voting power. With more shares outstanding after the merger, stockholder positions may be diluted. This is especially common with stock for stock mergers, where the new company hands out shares in exchange for shares of the former companies at a preset conversion rate (which is not always one for one).

ACQUISITIONS

Acquisitions take place when one company buys another. The acquiring company absorbs the target company into its business. Though acquisitions, sometimes called friendly takeovers, may be done at the agreement of the companies (as happens in a merger), one now owns the other. Unlike a merger, no new company emerges.

Ticker Trivia

A management acquisition occurs when a member of a corporation's current management team buys up a controlling interest in the company, basically turning it into a private corporation. These deals often involve a lot of debt financing, and require the approval of a majority of shareholders in order to go through.

To acquire a target company, the purchasing company buys up a majority share of the target firm's stock, often paying a tidy premium to existing shareholders. Neither company changes its name, and no new company shares are issued; both companies carry on as before, except that now the acquiring company owns the target corporation.

IMPACT ON SHAREHOLDERS

When one corporation acquires another, that action affects the shareholders of both companies, but in very different ways. On top of that, the way the acquiring company purchases the target company stocks can alter the effects on shareholders.

When the acquiring company uses money to get the target company's stock, share prices of each company changes. Right before the transaction is finalized, the price of the acquiring company normally drops. This dip is typically temporary, and the share price rebounds once the deal has gone through. On the other side, the stock price of the target company rises, because the acquiring company typically pays a premium to buy those shares.

But money is not the only way an acquiring company can purchase another firm. Stocks can be used, too. With a stock-for-stock transaction, the acquiring firm trades its stock for shares in the target firm. This then gives the target company's shareholders a stake in the acquiring company. For example, when ABC Corp. attempts to acquire XYZ Inc., it could offer current XYZ stockholders one share of ABC for every two shares of XYZ they own.

Further, acquisitions can also be done using a combination purchasing strategy: using a mix of stock and cash to obtain shares of the target company. For example, ABC could offer XYZ stockholders one share of ABC plus $5 for each share of XYZ they hold. This combined approach is the most common way acquisitions take place.

As for voting power, that will change for both sets of shareholders after the acquisition is finalized. While both will likely see their power diluted somewhat, shareholders of the target firm are usually impacted more. Especially with a stock-for-stock acquisition, which requires the issuance of additional shares, the proportion of shares any stockholder owns will shrink. For example, an ABC shareholder who previously owned a 3% stake in the company may see his holdings diluted to 2.25% after the issuance of the additional shares required to acquire XYZ.

DEALS DON'T ALWAYS WORK OUT

Most mergers and acquisitions are successful. Sometimes, though, deals fall through. This can happen for a few different reasons:

- One or both parties withdraw from the deal
- A regulatory body prohibits the deal
- The acquiring company can't find adequate financing
- Skeletons in the target company's closet are uncovered

It's not unusual for a company to put out feelers for mergers or acquisitions, then get cold feet. For example, change in board members or upper management can alter the company's direction and momentum, nixing plans for a potential combination. Shareholder resistance, economic shifts, and market swings can also affect upcoming deals.

When a prospective corporate merger or acquisition violates state or federal law, a regulatory body will come in and nix the deal. Most often, this happens when the new combination brushes up against antitrust or monopoly regulations. Written to protect consumers, these regulations strive to ensure market competition. Mergers or acquisitions that would create monopolies or severely limit competition for a particular industry are not allowed, but that doesn't mean that corporations don't try to slide such transactions through.

Funding issues are much more common with acquisitions than with mergers. When one corporation sets out to buy another, it has to purchase the takeover target's stock from current shareholders, always at an enticing premium over market price. These deals can run into billions of dollars, and acquiring companies can't always come up with the financing in time to see the deal through. In that case, the acquiring company withdraws from the transaction, and the deal does not go through.

Sometimes when an acquiring firm begins to dig deep into a target company's books, irregularities or hidden losses get uncovered. Under the skeptical eye of an ace accountant, for example, creative bookkeeping can come to light. The activity may not necessarily constitute illegal book cooking, but there may be inventive interpretations of the rules that cause profits to look bigger than they would be under more traditional accounting methods. Or perhaps the target company hasn't been fully forthcoming about unsuccessful research and development projects, potential lawsuits or scandals, or other deal breakers that the acquirer discovers during due diligence. Damaging skeletons in corporate closets can kill takeover transactions, if they're uncovered.

HOSTILE TAKEOVERS

Pirates Plunder the S.S. Megabucks

When a firm that is targeted for acquisition opposes the buyout attempt, it's called a hostile takeover. These deals can get downright nasty, as corporate raiders battle a resistant management team and board of directors. The enmity trickles down to the target firm's employees, stoking their loathing of the corporate conqueror and their expectations of getting fired in the aftermath. This pervasive animosity makes it almost impossible for the target of a hostile take-over to thrive after the deal is done.

Because it can be such a combative process, corporate raiders may sneak up on target companies. One example of this is the "dawn raid" maneuver. In this ambush, the investor (which can be a person or a company) stays under the radar, sending out buy orders for target company shares to various brokers, with instructions to purchase the stock at the opening bell. This strategy has a dual impact. The identity of the raider is hidden behind the brokers, so the target company board doesn't know who hit them. Because the stealth transaction takes place first thing, the company won't hear about the massive buy-up until it's too late. Plus, since the market doesn't have time to react and drive up the share price, the raider scoops up shares at the current price.

Another type of sneak attack that used to be more popular, until the U.S. government put a damper on it, is called the "Saturday night special." This strategy gets its name from the fact that the move is initiated over a weekend. This plot involves a public tender offer, where the acquiring party announces a willingness to buy shares at a premium. Their aim is to snap up a controlling interest before the target company has time to react. This scheme lost favor after the Williams Act was passed in 1968. The act basically requires that any corporate stock acquisition of 5% or more must be reported to the SEC.

Who Just Bought 5%?

Any time a person or company buys at least 5% of a corporation's stock, they have to file a form with the SEC, known as Schedule 13D, within ten days. Not only does the purchasing party have to identify himself (or itself, if it's a company), he also has to disclose quite a bit of information, such as any criminal past, why he bought the shares, and where he got the money to buy them.

BREAKING DOWN THE WILLIAMS ACT

The Williams Act was passed by Congress in 1968 to make sure that neither target companies nor their shareholders could be ambushed by an unwanted takeover. Under this law, the acquiring company is required to disclose their plans to the SEC and provide shareholders with a full disclosure.

As soon as any party acquires 5% of a corporation's shares, this act kicks in. When it does, the acquirer must report:

- The source of the funds being used to take over the target company
- The reason they want to buy the company
- What they plan to do with the company once they have a controlling interest
- Any contracts or agreements they have in place with the target company

Unfortunately, unscrupulous raiders find ways around this well-intentioned act. They can skirt the law by using derivative securities, like stock options, to accomplish their goals.

Whatever tactics they use to gobble up shares in the target company, the parties initiating a hostile takeover must have a lot of resources on hand. No matter what strategy they employ, the acquiring party almost always ends up paying more than the market price to garner a controlling interest.

In response to these underhanded stock grabs, target corporations have developed their own brand of tricks designed to keep raiders away. Those strategies fall under the category of shark repellent, and include imaginative tactics like poison pills, golden parachutes, and sandbags, which will be discussed later in more detail.

CORPORATE RAIDERS

Like the Vikings plundering village treasures, corporate raiders attack asset-rich corporations in an attempt to acquire them through a hostile takeover bid. But it takes more than a desire to pillage to become a successful corporate raider; it takes a lot of funding and a strong stomach.

To acquire his target, the raider tries to buy up enough shares of the corporation to gain a controlling interest. Because he doesn't have the approval of the target company's board of directors, he has to circumvent them. If he can't grab enough shares to succeed, the raider may appeal directly to the company's shareholders, asking them to sell their shares for a premium.

Despite their zeal for snapping up shares and adding corporations to their holdings, raiders typically don't intend to keep the companies they acquire. Rather, these calculating businessmen look to make enormous, quick profits by chopping the companies up and selling off their valuable assets. For that reason, they zero in on corporations that have undervalued assets, meaning that what the target company owns is worth more than the market realizes.

For example, Big Money Corporation has a million shares on the market with a current stock price of $10, for a total $10 million market value. To keep things simple, suppose Big Money has no debt and a lot of cash on hand, $2 million, and other assets on the books totaling $8 million. The market value of those assets, though, is currently $15 million. That would make Big Money Corporation desirable prey for a corporate raider, because the company's assets are undervalued by $5 million.

BARBARIANS AT THE GATE

Spurred by unbridled arrogance and insatiable greed, one larger-than-life CEO set out to line his pockets by wielding his corporate power. This true-life drama inspired the 1993 film *Barbarians at the Gate*, but the real story eclipses the fictional plot.

The story begins back in the 1980s, when cigarettes were attracting more lawsuits than new smokers. R.J. Reynolds Tobacco Company came under pressure and was facing a very precarious future. Conservative and cost-conscious CEO J. Tylee Wilson began to put out feelers for a potential merger. After careful consideration and a lot of advice, Wilson landed on Nabisco Brands, led by F. Ross Johnson, the villain of our tale.

Johnson had come from Standard Brands, where under his reign as CEO his salary tripled, and corporate jets and luxury cars were added to the executive perks, all with the approval of the board. Standard Brands merged with Nabisco back in 1981, creating Nabisco Brands, and Johnson soon found himself, once again, in the top spot, where he promptly set out to curry favor among the board members. Then, once again, he used the corporate checkbook to fund his lavish lifestyle and line his personal pockets, with no objections from the board.

The two disparate executives finally met in the spring of 1985 to discuss the merger they both wanted. With a much longer and stronger background, Wilson intended to act as chairman of the newly formed company with Johnson his second in command. Johnson wasn't really interested in being a vice chairman, opting instead for a more active role in the corporation as its president and COO. The deal finally went through, with R.J. Reynolds buying Nabisco Brands for a record-breaking $4.9 billion (the largest amount ever paid for a non-oil company). As Wilson and Johnson began to work together at RJR Nabisco, their contrasting styles became quickly apparent. Johnson, in his usual style, cozied up to the board members, and began to turn them against Wilson. In less than one year, Johnson was top dog and enjoying a huge salary with lavish perks.

Then, in 1987, RJR Nabisco stock suffered a one-two punch. The market crash hit their share price hard, and at the same time tobacco products were falling out of favor with consumers. Always looking out for himself, Johnson started to search for new ways to bring in money that wouldn't involve anyone looking over his shoulder. Interested in the benefits of a leveraged buyout (LBO), Johnson connected with expert Henry Kravis from KKR (Kohlberg Kravis & Roberts), who was very interested in pursuing the deal to buy RJR Nabisco. At the same time, behind his back, Johnson was secretly working with another investment bank, Shearson Lehman Hutton.

In this deal, Johnson insisted on receiving 20% of the company stock (for himself and some other top management personnel) and complete control of the board, virtually the definition of a black knight attempting a hostile takeover.

A bidding battle broke out between KKR (who wanted nothing more to do with Johnson) and Shearson Lehman (still working with Johnson). First came a bid for $75 a share from Johnson's team, then $90 from KKR, and the bids climbed higher and higher as RJR Nabisco board members watched. All of a sudden, a gray knight appeared; out of nowhere, First Boston bid $118 per share. But when the financing for that fell through, the board decided to accept KKR's $109 per share bid even though it was slightly lower than the bid from Shearson Lehman. The deal finally closed for another record-breaking amount, $25 billion.

KKR kicked Johnson out of his post at the company, but Johnson still won in the end. As part of his contract, Johnson walked away with his golden parachute intact, leaving RJR Nabisco with $30 million.

KNIGHTS OF MANY COLORS

In a medieval twist, some parties to takeovers are known as knights.

Just like in old tales of castles, princesses, and round tables, the black knights are the bad guys. Here, these corporate raiders seek to take over a resistant company that does not want to be bought in what is known as a hostile takeover attempt.

White knights ride in to the rescue, offering the target company a way out of the hostile takeover. This corporate savior gives the company a chance for a friendly takeover instead.

A yellow knight starts out as a black knight, attempting a hostile takeover. Midway through the process, this party switches up his strategy and begins to negotiate with the target company, hoping to resolve the matter to benefit both sides.

Sometimes when an acquiring party and a target company are in the middle of talks, a gray knight rides in with his own bid, out of the blue.

PROXY FIGHTS

An all-out battle among stockholders of the target company is called a proxy fight. Like other facets of hostile takeovers, proxy fights can get downright ugly.

Investors in favor of the takeover attempt to bring the other shareholders around to their side, persuading them to approve the action. They accomplish that by getting the shareholders' proxies, the right act on behalf of those shareholders in an upcoming vote. If the raiding party scoops up enough proxies, they win, and the takeover goes through—even if the board of directors is opposed to it.

Ticker Trivia

Proxy fights can also be initiated by concerned active shareholders who are looking to make changes in the direction of the corporation, or in the board of directors themselves.

Companies concerned about potential takeover attempts may decide to issue different kinds of shares: some with fewer voting rights, and others with more voting rights. The shares with fewer voting rights may pay a higher dividend rate to make them more attractive to investors. These are called DVRs (differential voting rights). Holders of DVR shares may, for example, get one vote for every hundred shares they own. This strategy, which can make it more difficult for a raider to get enough votes, is gaining popularity among potential target corporations.

TENDER OFFERS

Sometimes a corporate raider will go directly to the source to buy target company stock: the current shareholders. In a move called a tender offer, the raider promises to buy their shares at a fixed price that's greater than the current market price.

For example, if shares in ABC, Inc. were trading for $10 per share, the raider would pledge to pay ABC stockholders $12 per share if they sold directly to him. That $2 difference is the premium over market price, a cost of doing business for the corporate raider.

There is a catch, however. Enough shareholders must agree to the deal, enough to give the raider a controlling interest, or the sale will not go through.

GREENMAIL

Similar to blackmail, greenmail is used by a corporate raider to force a target company to buy back its own shares at highly inflated prices in order to prevent a hostile takeover. It begins with a corporate raider buying up target company shares, accumulating enough stock to become a viable threat.

Once the target company board realizes its position, the raider announces the greenmail demand. The target corporation is then forced to buy their shares from the raider, at a significant premium over the market price so that they can save their company, and thus thwart the takeover attempt.

SHARK REPELLENT

Corporate raiders act like pillagers, striking fat targets with the speed and precision of a shark. To fend them off, targeted companies need strong shark repellent. That is, they need a collection of strategies designed to deter even the most voracious predator.

Take the sandbag defense, for example. With this tactic, the target company tries to stall the raider, hoping to get a better offer from a more favorable party, called a white knight. The managers of a target company must strike a fine balance here, as they attempt to keep the raider at bay and entice a white knight to come to their rescue—all while they're still running the company.

Or consider the Pac-Man defense, where the target company turns the tables and gobbles up shares of the acquiring company. Another inventive tactic called the crown jewel defense involves the target company's most valuable assets. In the case of a hostile takeover, the corporate bylaws state that those most valuable assets must be sold, and the acquiring company would be legally forced to comply, selling off the very things it was after in the first place.

Poison Pills

In an attempt to thwart an impending hostile takeover, a target corporation may employ a poison pill strategy. This tactic is designed to make the company appear unattractive so that the raider loses interest. The tricky part: not making the company so unattractive that its share price never recovers (insiders call that situation a "suicide pill").

The two most common poison pill strategies are flip-in and flip-over, and each has a direct impact on the company's investors.

With a flip-in poison pill, the company's existing shareholders (other than the party attempting the takeover) can buy up more shares for a discounted price. This serves a dual purpose: weakening the acquirer's stock position and making the deal more painful and pricey for him. Suppose the acquirer has just obtained 5% of the outstanding shares. When the flip-in is enacted, more shares come onto the market. That dilutes his 5% holding and his power. On top of that, he now has to pick up even more shares to gain a controlling interest, making this a more expensive takeover than expected. This strategy is often included in the shareholder rights plan of the target corporation.

This poison pill tactic was implemented in 2012 by Netflix (albeit unsuccessfully) to ward off the takeover by famed investor Carl Icahn. When Icahn announced that he had bought up almost 10% of the corporation's shares, Netflix quickly established a shareholder rights plan that stated the board of directors would let current shareholders snap up newly issued Netflix shares for less than the stock's market price if anyone purchased at least 10% of the company.

Ticker Trivia

In the event of a hostile takeover, the "people pill" strategy calls for the walkout of key personnel.

The flip-over poison pill plan is less commonly used. This strategy lets the shareholders of the target company buy stock in the acquiring company for a bargain basement price. Since this provision is written into the target company's shareholder rights plan, the acquiring company has to honor it, even at the expense of its existing shareholders.

Golden Parachutes

Golden parachutes are among the most controversial forms of shark repellent. The strategy is designed to ward off potential raiders by promising extremely lucrative payouts to the current corporate bigwigs, executives like the CEO (chief executive officer) and CFO (chief financial officer). Often, these top dogs lose their positions in the event of a corporate takeover, and the golden parachute ensures they'll land softly when their jobs are gone.

Typically, golden parachutes are part of executive employment contracts. They can include benefits such as:

- Stock options
- Cash bonuses
- Huge severance packages
- Continuing perks (like company cars)
- Outplacement services

These golden parachutes often deliver millions of dollars' worth of benefits to those executives, and the acquiring company will be on the hook to pay them out, making the takeover target much more expensive.

Why the controversy? Golden parachutes reward top executives, often at the expense of the shareholders.

The Macaroni Defense

Another strategy an unwilling target company can employ to deter would-be takeover attempts is known as the macaroni defense. To accomplish this, the company issues bonds that come with a very special pledge: If the company is taken over, the bonds must be redeemed for even more money. Basically, in the case of a hostile acquisition, the corporate debt expands—in much the same way that macaroni expands when you throw it in boiling water. To really make an impact, though, the bond issue has to be large enough to scare off the raider.

The downside to the macaroni defense is increased debt and the expense of interest payments. Even when the tactic successfully stops a takeover, it leaves the target company saddled with this new large liability.

ESOPs

Another way to preempt a hostile takeover involves corporate forethought, and the implementation of an employee stock ownership plan, or ESOP. ESOPs are a type of retirement plan, like 401(k)s and other such plans, and an ESOP provides tax benefits for everyone involved.

When a corporation creates an ESOP, they give their employees stock in the company, stacking the deck against would-be corporate raiders. People who own a stake in the company they work for are far more likely to vote with familiar, trusted company management than with an invading outsider.

Thousands of publicly traded corporations employing millions of workers maintain ESOPs, and some of those companies are at least 50% owned by their employees. Examples include Publix Super Markets (based in Florida), with a roster of 175,000 employees, and Davey Tree Expert (based in Ohio), which boasts 8,300 employees in the United States.

BUYING AND SELLING

Rule No 1: Don't Lose Money

Most educators will tell you that 75% of all learning is gained by doing homework. This is true of investing as well. When you are interested in investing, it's important that you do your homework in the form of research, analysis, and investigation. Use the Internet to look up the stock you own and find any company news listings. Read the company newsletter, its annual or semiannual reports, and ask your broker for any updated news about the company. An educated investor is more likely to be a patient and relaxed investor.

KNOW WHAT YOU'RE BUYING, BUY WHAT YOU KNOW

One of the benefits of being a consumer is that you are called on to evaluate products and services every day. You have learned that you can get the best results by thoroughly researching your options before you make a purchasing decision. Maybe you've recently purchased some new electronics that you just can't put down, switched cereal brands to cut some of the sugar out of your kids' diet, or started a new medication that actually made you feel better without any side effects. You can put your experiences as a savvy consumer to work when you're making your investment decisions.

Your observations are another way to gain valuable insight. During your recent trip to Japan, did you notice people consuming huge quantities of a new Coca-Cola product? While waiting to pay for dinner at your favorite restaurant, did you notice that many of the patrons pulled out American Express cards? Part of doing your homework as an investor is noticing the products and services that are prominently displayed and used by the people around you.

Ticker Trivia

Putting serious thought into your investments early on will most likely pay off in the long run. Unfortunately, many people are introduced to the world of investing through a hot stock tip from their barber, buddy, or bellman. There's really no way to make an easy buck, and jumping into a stock because of a random tip will probably cause you to lose money.

Another huge consideration when buying stocks is price. Would you pay any amount to buy a car or a house? Probably not. Most people like to feel that they've gotten a good deal. They're looking for a price that's proportionate to their buying budget and what they get from the purchase. It's the same with stock investing: The price of a particular stock is a critical part of the buying and selling equation. Taking a business attitude toward stock buying is important—it is wise to base your investment decisions on a variety of factors, including purchase price. That's the only way to ensure profitability in the long run. You want high quality at a fair (or better than fair) price.

Fortunately, good-quality companies in this country are plentiful. Finding these companies, however, is something of a challenge. Some investors are more inclined to look for the current hot stock, while others prefer to hunt out a great deal. Growth investing and value investing are two common approaches. (Earlier chapters offer more detailed information about these approaches.)

GET THE FACTS

Both styles of investing can be lucrative. The idea is to figure out which style of investment better fits your personality and investment strategy. Sometimes you may lean toward growth investing; other times, you may feel that taking a value-investing approach is the way to go. Still other times you may want growth and value all wrapped up in one neat package. In that case, you would be looking for growth at a reasonable price, known in industry lingo as GARP.

Checklist

Every investor should use a research checklist to evaluate stock under consideration. Look for annual reports, financial statements, industry comparisons, and current news items. Analyze your findings before making investment decisions. Once you become a shareholder, you will find that your main information needs can be fulfilled with press releases, ongoing financial statements, and judicious stock price monitoring.

Whichever style you choose, you need a place to get the information on which you can base your decision. These days, there's no better starting point than the Internet. On the web, you can easily find the best investment information in real time, mostly for free. More and more, investors both young and old are turning to websites to limit their reliance on expensive financial advisors. In addition to the prospect company's web page, there are dozens of sites that provide in-depth company data, and even more sites offer real-time stock quotes.

There is no shortage of good market research available to you as an investor. Part of your job is to determine which sources work best for your needs.

TWO PROVEN WAYS
TO ANALYZE STOCKS

Investors generally favor one of two stock-picking techniques: technical analysis or fundamental analysis. Technical analysis is all about stock prices and how they move, and it relies on charts and graphs to determine patterns. Fundamental analysis, more common among beginning investors, involves studying the company itself, with a focus on financial statements and performance. For optimum results, many savvy investors combine both techniques when making trade decisions. For example, a stock with great fundamentals and sagging price trends could indicate trouble on the horizon.

What's a Good First Step in Selecting Stocks?

Learn about all the products and/or services offered by the company you're considering. A company may have one high-profile product and several other products and/or services that are not as visible. Even if a high-profile product is getting rave reviews and profits, the company's lesser-known products may be taking a toll on the total profits—or vice versa.

Technical analysis focuses on charts and graphs showing past stock prices and volume patterns. There are a number of patterns technical analysts recognize to be historically recurring. The trick is to identify the pattern before it is completed, and then buy or sell according to where the pattern indicates the stock is headed. Those who use this technique believe you can forecast future stock prices by studying past price trends. They make trades based primarily on stock price movements. Technical analysts tend to do much more buying and selling than fundamental analysts.

Fundamental analysis is a long-used, common way to review stocks. The technique involves an analysis of the company's ability to generate earnings and an examination of the value of the company's total assets. Value investing and growth investing are two subdivisions of fundamental analysis. Proponents of fundamental analysis believe that stock prices will rise as a result of growth. Earnings, dividends, and book values are all examined, and a buy-and-hold approach is usually followed. Advocates of fundamental analysis maintain that stock in well-run, high-quality companies will become more valuable over time.

KNOW WHEN TO SELL

Knowing when to hold and when to sell a particular stock is an art in itself. You may have every intention of sticking with your investments for the long haul, but maybe the first sign of turbulence sends you into a panic to sell. History has revealed that holding on to solid stocks for a minimum of five to ten years has produced the best results. Therefore, buying good companies and holding them for the long term is a sound strategy for most investors.

When you decided to buy your stock, you thoroughly researched its balance sheet, income statement, and ratio analyses. The same holds true when you're thinking of selling a stock. Before you jump on a sell bandwagon because of something you see on the news or hear at the water cooler, reevaluate your holdings carefully. If the share value is still growing, selling too soon can mean you will miss out on additional profits. At the same time, though, you don't want to hold on to a losing stock. Selling at the wrong time can easily destroy your investing plan, so don't do it on impulse. And don't worry about losing your shirt; there's a simple way to make sure that doesn't happen.

The primary way to lock in your profits and limit your losses is with a standing stop-loss order. A stop-loss order is a specialized instruction to your broker that tells him to sell a stock when its price has declined by a certain percentage. A stop loss can be placed based on the original buy price, or it can move with the stock price (called a trailing stop). Here's how it works: Suppose you buy a stock for $10 per share. You want to limit your losses to 10%. You would place a stop order for $9 per share, which means that if the share price fell to $9, your broker would automatically sell the stock.

With a trailing stop, the sell price increases proportionally when the stock price goes up, helping you both limit losses and lock in already earned profits. Suppose you bought that same $10 stock, and you want a 10% loss limit. When the stock goes up to $15.00, your trailing stop increases to $13.50, 10% less than the new share price.

EXECUTING STOCK TRADES

The Nuts and Bolts of Trading

As an individual investor in the stock market, your first concern is how to go about executing a stock trade. Fortunately, it's usually as simple as picking up the phone or clicking the mouse. For example, if you trade through a broker, you can simply call and place an order for 100 shares of any company, like IBM. Almost immediately, you'll get confirmation that your order has been filled and that you now own stock in IBM. When you make your own online trades, you simply follow the point-and-click instructions on the brokerage website to execute your trade. A confirmation should follow almost immediately.

Of course, things can get a little more complicated, as there are several different types of stock orders. Your options include a market order (like the IBM example), a limit order, and a stop order (which includes a stop order buy, and a stop order sell). You can also determine the length of time your order is in effect. For example, you can specify that the order is only good for the specific day on which it is placed.

MARKET ORDER

When you want to buy or sell a stock at the current market price, you place a market order. This means you want to buy or sell a stock at whatever price the stock is trading for when your order reaches the floor. In other words, you're buying or selling a given stock at the going rate. Depending on whether you're buying or selling, the market price may differ. The broker's terms for these prices are the bid (buy) or ask (sell), and the difference between these two prices is known as the spread. For example, IBM's bid price (the amount some-one is willing to pay) may be $114.25, while its asking price (the amount someone is willing to accept) is $114.50. In this case, the spread is twenty-five cents.

A Good Price Barometer

Get an idea of the fifty-two-week highs and lows of the stocks you're looking to purchase and use this to set target prices for when to sell. As the stock approaches the target price you can start selling off shares, and then gauge to what degree you believe it might pass the target. Don't use the target as an absolute figure but as a barometer.

Unlike IBM, securities that are thinly (infrequently) traded often have bigger spreads. Dealers in a security generally keep a large part of the spread in exchange for playing the role of middleman. Like all middle-men, dealers are in the business of selling goods at a higher price than what they initially paid. Stock prices, especially in heavily traded stock, can change in just seconds. By the time your order is filled with a market order, you might find a slight difference in the price you were quoted.

When you place the order, you can specify a particular time frame during which the trade can be executed. Standard order periods include:

- Day orders, which are either filled or automatically expire by the end of the trading day
- Minute orders, which expire as soon as the specified number of minutes have passed

- GTD (good-til-date) orders, which stay active until they are either filled or canceled
- GTC (good-til-canceled) orders, which stay open until they are executed or canceled
- AON (all-or-none) orders, which must be filled in their entirety or they get canceled at the end of the trading day
- FOK (fill-or-kill) orders, which have to be filled instantly and entirely or not at all
- IOC (immediate-or-cancel) orders, which are canceled if not filled instantly, either entirely or partially

These time frames can be applied to market orders and limit orders, and are used to give the investor more ways to control the execution of his stock trades.

LIMIT ORDER

Limit orders are placed if you don't want to purchase stock for more or sell a stock for less than a predetermined price. A limit order, like other types of orders, can be placed as a day order or as a GTC (good-til-canceled) order. Your limit order may not fill with either one of these two options. However, you have a greater chance of your order being filled with a GTC order since it can remain open for a longer period of time.

If you want to buy a stock for a specified price, you can place a limit buy order. Let's say Amazon.com (AMZN) is currently trading at $710. You want to buy 100 shares of Amazon, but only if it dips to $700. In this case, you place a limit order for 100 shares of Amazon at $700 per share. The order will fill for $700 per share if the price dips to that level (or lower). If it does not, your order will remain unfilled. Your order to buy stock may also be filled for less than $700 per share if the stock hits $700 and continues to drop. If that happens, your order would fill at the first available price under $700. This happens because prices often move more quickly than trades can be settled. One thing is for certain, though: Your order will not fill for more than $700 per share.

Now let's say you own stock in Amazon.com, and you bought it at $700 per share. To lock in profits, you might decide to place a limit order to sell your shares if the stock price climbs to $750 per share. In this case, your order will fill for at least $750 per share, though it could be filled for more than that amount if the stock price hits $750 and continues to rise. In this beneficial circumstance, your stock would be sold at the first opportunity at $750 or higher; again, stock prices usually move faster than sell orders can settle. However, your order to sell those Amazon.com shares will not fill for less than $750 per share.

Be aware, though, that brokers typically charge a higher commission to fulfill a limit order than to execute a market order. That offset can eat away at gains, so it's important to factor that in when setting limit prices.

STOP ORDER

Stop orders (also called stop-loss orders) are crucial for investors who are concerned about a stock's price falling too low, and want to lock in profits or limit losses. Using either a fixed dollar amount or a percentage, the investor sets a stop point; that is, a price at which the stock is automatically put up for sale. This strategy takes the emotion out of making critical trading decisions. When this type of order is entered, once your stock reaches the stop point, the order transforms into a market order.

Stop Order Buy

To get in on a stock rally at the exact point you want in, you can place a stop order to buy. Let's say Intel (INTC) is currently selling at $19 per share. If the price climbs to $22, you'd like to buy it because you think the price will continue to rise. Therefore, you put in a stop order to buy at $22. Once Intel hits $22 per share, your stop order automatically becomes a market order. Your order might be filled at your stop point of $22. However, since the stop order becomes a market order at your set stop point, you might also end up paying more or less for the stock. The price might rise to $22.50, for instance, before your order is filled. Conversely, the stock might hit $22 and then drop; you might end up buying it for $21.50.

Stop Order Sell

Let's say you bought that Intel stock at $22 per share. You can now place a stop order to sell if the stock price drops to $20. Once the stock hits your set stop point, called a hard stop, your stop order to sell becomes a market order. Again, that means your order might end up being filled at a higher or lower price, depending on the market price at the time your order is filled.

Another way to lock in profits is with a trailing stop, which sets the stop point as a percentage of the price as it's rising, then kicks in when the price falls. For example, a 10% trailing stop for a stock trading at $22 would be $2.20, so a sell order would kick in if the stock fell to $19.80. If the stock price rose, though, the sell point would rise with it. For example, if the price climbed to $30 per share, a fall down to $27 per share (a loss of 10%) would trigger a sale.

STOCKBROKERS

May I Take Your Order?

As an investor, you have multiple options for choosing a stockbroker. Before you make your selection, you need to evaluate your needs, comfort level, personal commitment, and available time for research, as well as your desire to be personally involved in your investment portfolio. Also be sure you are aware of any fees associated with your choice of broker and service level.

At the most basic level, a broker simply fills your orders and does nothing else, so that's all you pay for. As you move up in service levels from there, you'll notice fees and costs climbing as well. And while virtually every type of broker offers some form of online account access, which may include trades, that doesn't make them all online brokers.

DISCOUNT BROKERS

If you are ready, willing, and able to investigate potential companies on your own, then a discount broker may fit the bill. Many individuals find that taking charge of their investments is an empowering experience. Once they become acquainted with all of the available information, many investors feel like they are in the best position to handle their own investments, and are happy to be in the driver's seat.

Commissions charged by brokerage houses were deregulated in 1975, and this decision was truly the beginning of the ascent of the discount broker. Trades could be conducted for far less money than investors were used to paying at full-service brokerage firms. Discount brokers are now offering more services than ever before. Combine that with today's new and faster technology, and investors have all of the investment information they need right at their disposal.

Online-only brokers are available only on the Internet; there is no option to walk into a traditional broker's office and talk with someone face-to-face. Online brokers are expanding the range of services they offer over the Internet and are starting to catch up with full-service brokers in areas like research assistance and personalized trading advice.

With ever-accelerating developments on the Internet, the opportunity for self-education keeps improving. Beginning investors now have access to many of the same resources as full-service brokers. With this access to data, the demand for full-service brokers is diminishing. A little enthusiasm and determination on your part can pay off. With the wealth of online information, you can stay informed on everything from a company's new product rollouts to the ten most highly traded stocks on any given day. You can also get real-time quotes and in-depth analyses.

The proliferation of online discount brokers has made it possible to trade around the clock for a nominal fee. In some cases, you can make trades for under $10. Trading online is ideal if you have done your homework and know exactly which stock you want to own.

FULL-SERVICE BROKERS

If you want someone else to do most of the legwork, you might opt for a full-service broker. Of course, full-service brokers charge a premium for their input. There is no guarantee that a full-service broker will steer you in the direction of massive capital gains. It is also true that many such brokers tend to pay more attention to their large accounts (clients investing more than $250,000, for example) than the smaller ones.

Know Who You're Trusting

If you want to work with a full-service broker, get a reference from someone you know and trust who has actually used his financial services. Don't rely on a referral from someone who knows the broker professionally, but who hasn't ever relied on his financial advice.

Some experts believe that if you have investments totaling more than $100,000, you may want to explore the possibility of at least consulting a full-service broker. If you decide to do that, find a broker who both shares your basic investment philosophy and gives you several investment options to choose from. Choose a broker with extensive investment experience and a track record trading in both bull and bear markets. Most important, make sure you feel comfortable with the broker personally, and that he is willing to listen to your input, and answer all your questions without hesitation.

It's perfectly acceptable (and advisable) to interview potential brokers. Ask how long they have been in this business and inquire about their formal education and investment philosophy. Find out if they rely only on their brokerage firm's reports when making stock recommendations. You can also ask more pointed questions, like how their clients fared during a recent downturn, or what strategies they use to protect their clients from losses. Also make sure the broker provides you upfront with a written list of fees you'll be charged, along with an explanation of when charges will be incurred. If the broker gives you the runaround or refuses to answer your questions, find someone else to work with.

MONITORING THE BROKERS

Becoming acquainted with the broker fee structure is crucial. In many cases, you may be charged for services you didn't know you were getting—and wouldn't use even if you knew you could. You also want to inquire about the fees associated with opening, maintaining, and closing an account; getting checks; participating in investment profiles; buying and selling securities; and attending various seminars. To circumvent potential discrepancies, it's important that you obtain this information in writing and in advance—and not after the fact.

The Financial Industry Regulatory Authority (FINRA) can answer your questions about the practices of a particular broker by looking up his past record regarding any disciplinary actions taken or complaints that have been registered against him. They can also confirm whether the broker is licensed to conduct business in your state.

Another Way to Protect Investors

FINRA (Financial Industry Regulatory Authority) was created in July 2007 when the National Association of Securities Dealers (NASD) merged with the regulation committee of the NYSE. Before that, NASD took the lead with consumer-broker issues. The NASD also had primary responsibility for the running of the NASDAQ exchange and other over-the-counter markets, as well as administering licensing exams for financial professionals.

In addition to being the primary nongovernmental agency dedicated to protecting the investing public, FINRA also regulates every securities firm that operates in the United States—more than 5,000 firms. To get the job done, FINRA employs about 3,600 professionals in sixteen offices throughout the United States, with its main offices in New York City and Washington, D.C.

PROTECT YOURSELF FROM DISHONEST BROKERS

The vast majority of stockbrokers operate with integrity, but there are also a lot of scammers out there who are looking to score profits at the expense of investors. The SEC and FINRA do their best to track down swindlers, but they can't catch them all. Your best defense against broker fraud is due diligence and personal references.

Even thorough background checks can't smoke out every scam artist, especially when it's so very easy for them to create realistic websites that mirror those of well-respected investment firms. So after you've done your homework, pay attention to what your broker does and how he treats you. The dishonest ones will use tricks to increase their commissions, urge you to buy sham investments, even funnel funds out of your account. If you know what to look for, though, you won't be caught with a drained brokerage account.

One nasty trick to look out for is called churning. Brokers who engage in churning make trades in your account purely for the sake of generating commissions. Churning especially benefits brokers who work on straight commission—the more trades they make, the more pay they take home. The impact on your portfolio can be devastating: Excessive commissions eat away at your funds while the value of your investments decreases. Any trade that has no reasonable purpose is a churn trade, even if it happens just once. If you notice trades in your account that don't make sense, contact your broker immediately, before it can happen again.

FINANCIAL PLANNERS

If you need all-around money management advice, consider hiring a professional financial planner. These people go beyond handling your investments—they aid you in matters relating to insurance, taxes, trusts, and real estate. The cost of doing business with a financial planner can vary considerably. If you opt for a financial planner, consider hiring a fee-based planner rather than a commission-based planner. If the planner works on commission alone, it may be in her best interest to encourage heavy trading. While some planners charge a flat hourly rate, others may charge a fee that is based on your total assets and trading activity. In this type of arrangement, you are responsible for paying the financial planner even if you do not follow any of her suggestions. Other planners operate with a combination of fee-based charges and commission. Here, you may pay less per trade, but you are also responsible for paying additional fees.

INVESTMENT CLUBS

Safety in Numbers

Buying a wide variety of stocks can be cost-prohibitive for individual investors. Some turn to mutual funds or exchange-traded funds, but others like to have more control over where their investing dollars wind up, and those people form investment clubs.

When a group of people get together, pool their money, and use it to make investments, you've got an investment club. Technically speaking, investment clubs are usually set up as partnerships or limited liability companies (LLCs), with official rules and bylaws governing funds, investments, and withdrawals. On average, investment clubs tend to have ten to twenty members. At this size they are large enough to be able to afford a diverse pool of securities, and small enough to keep things friendly and manageable.

To get started, each member ponies up an initial lump sum. Most times, all group members put up the same amount, but as long as there are clear records and all members are in agreement, contributions may vary. After that, members pay in a monthly contribution, usually ranging from $50 to $100, to be put toward additional investments.

Once there's a pool of money for purchasing, the real fun begins. Each member of an investment group plays his part by studying a specific stock (or two) in great detail, and then presents his findings to the group. Then, the group votes to decide which investments to buy, and later which to hold and which to sell. Generally, each club member actively participates in all investment decisions, which make the group's agreed-upon investing time frame and style very important.

Clubs normally meet about once a month, and members can include your neighbors, coworkers, friends, and relatives. To make for a cohesive group, members should share similar investment philosophies. Some of the most successful clubs witness the best results when members develop a comprehensive investment strategy and stick with it. Such an undertaking is a great way for new investors to get acquainted with basic investing techniques and for experienced investors to sharpen their skills. Members can share ideas and learn from each other's mistakes.

TIME MATTERS

The best investment clubs succeed because they have clear plans and a long-term time frame. That goes for both the investments themselves and the club members.

Getting in and out of stock positions can be costly, and trying to time the market with monthly votes can lead to disastrous losses. For the best success, clubs should focus more on the companies they invest in, and less on monthly changes in stock prices. By using stop orders, profits can be locked in, and losses limited. This, in turn, frees club members to focus on new investment opportunities and long-term growth.

Club members should commit to a long-term time frame as well, agreeing to participate for at least three to five years. In addition, the group should agree on withdrawal notification procedures, as early withdrawals can severely affect the group's portfolio. To temper sudden decisions to pull out, many clubs impose penalties on members who drop out earlier than originally agreed upon, which must be paid at the time they withdraw their funds. This helps offset the extra costs involved with liquidating a stock position to pay out the withdrawn funds.

A COMMON STYLE

Blue chips, growth stocks, penny stocks, foreign stocks: it's important for members to agree on the core investing style and goals for their investment club. With a defined style, it will be much easier to analyze and compare investment options. A defined style also makes it much simpler to design a profitable portfolio.

When members choose stocks to present to the group, those securities should fall within the club guidelines. To enhance clarity, the club can set acceptable ranges for share prices (for example, no stocks costing more than $20 per share or less than $8 per share), market capitalization, and market sectors (for example, no one sector can make up more than 15% of the portfolio). By defining specific criteria for stocks in the group portfolio, the club will be more likely to meet its goals, and members will have a better understanding of the types of stocks that are appropriate for recommendation.

Experienced investment club advisors suggest that members invest a set amount on an ongoing basis, reinvest dividends their shares earn, and invest in a variety of different stocks that fit the club's goals. By investing so regularly, clubs make good use of dollar-cost averaging, which means investing a predetermined sum of money on an ongoing basis as opposed to making an investment in one lump sum. Using this method, the club gets more shares for its money when a stock's price goes down. On the flip side, the group receives fewer shares for that fixed amount when the stock's price increases. The regular fixed-sum investing helps balance out fluctuations in share prices.

BETTER INVESTING

For more than fifty years, BetterInvesting (formerly known as the National Association of Investors Corporation, or NAIC) has been helping investment clubs get up and running. And those efforts have certainly paid off. Due to the growing popularity of investing over the past several years, the organization has witnessed a dramatic increase in its membership.

This Madison Heights, Michigan, not-for-profit organization provides members of the BetterInvesting community with an information-packed brochure called "How to Start an Investment Club" and a robust online curriculum to help get investors started. The organization's monthly magazine, *BetterInvesting*, covers a wide array of investment-related topics. In addition, members have access to sample agreements and brochures. To join, there is a nominal annual fee per club, plus a fee for each club member.

BetterInvesting.org

The BetterInvesting website offers a variety of free educational resources including webinars, 24/7 market data, research tools, and even commission-free stock trades for registered investment groups. Visit www.betterinvesting .org to learn more.

IPOS

The Ground Floor

Initial public offerings, or IPOs, mark the first time stock in a corporation is made available to the public; that's why IPOs are referred to as "going public." This undertaking helps small, young, privately owned companies obtain the financing they need to expand their businesses.

IPOs can be very complex and intricate. There are a lot of rules and regulations governing both the underwriters and the issuers. However, there are some basic steps all IPOs follow.

First, the company going public, now called the issuer, works with an underwriter to figure out all the details, which includes what types of shares they will issue, how many, the best offering price, and the optimal timing.

Underwriters

An underwriter raises investment capital on behalf of the company that is issuing an IPO. Typically these underwriters are banks or large financial institutions.

Next, the preliminary registration documents are prepared and filed with the proper governing bodies, including the SEC. This paperwork contains crucial information about the offering and about the company along with filing details, that include things like current financial statements, information about key management personnel, how they plan to use the money they raise, and how much stock will be held by company insiders.

While the SEC confirms the information in those documents, a time frame called the "cooling off period," the underwriter creates a preliminary prospectus to generate interest in the offering.

When the SEC signs off on the offering, finalized documents and a final prospectus are submitted for approval. This set of papers includes the official offering date, known as the effective date, when the shares can finally be sold. That final prospectus is legally binding, and it includes the firm offering price for the IPO shares. This is the only time that a stock price is fixed. Once they hit the secondary market, stock prices are determined by investor sentiment—whatever amount someone is willing to pay.

IPO DEAL STRUCTURES

When underwriting an IPO, there are two main ways to structure the deal. Under the terms of a "best efforts" agreement, the underwriter sells the offering company's securities, but does not guarantee the amount of money that will be raised. A "firm commitment" structure, on the other hand, means that the underwriter has guaranteed that a specific amount of capital will be raised. They do that by buying the entire offering, then reselling it to public investors.

Most of the time, IPOs are underwritten by a group of investment banks; that group is called a syndicate. Operating with a group helps spread the risk of the IPO among underwriters, so no one company carries the full weight of the offering.

RED HERRINGS AND THE DOG AND PONY SHOW

When a company is ready to go public, but the SEC hasn't yet given them the green light, its owners and their underwriter still have a lot of work to do. They have to get enough high-level investors interested in the shares they're offering to fund their corporation.

That starts with a "red herring," the colorful name given to the preliminary prospectus. This document contains virtually all the information about the company and its upcoming IPO except for a few key pieces of information: the offering price and the effective date.

With their red herring in hand, the company bigwigs and the underwriter go on the road, meeting with potential investors in an attempt to get them excited about investing in the new corporation. This road show is called the "dog and pony show," and it's a very important part of the IPO process. Without enough enthusiasm and anticipation surrounding the offering, they may not be able to raise enough capital to fully fund their venture.

ADVANCED INVESTING TECHNIQUES

Don't Try This at Home

For investors who love the thrill of high risk and the potential of increased rewards, margin buying and short selling can fulfill those itches. These techniques are not suitable for conservative, risk-averse investors, or for investors who really can't afford to lose money. This is because when you employ these strategies, you cross the line from investing into gambling, and you can lose even more than your original investment.

MARGIN BUYING

In the world of stock trading, margin buying means borrowing money to purchase stocks. Sounds simple, but it can get complicated very quickly, especially if the market moves suddenly in an unexpected direction. Margin buying can amplify investment gains and losses, which makes it a valuable but highly risky strategy.

Margin buying requires that you have a brokerage account that holds your investments, or at least some of them. The brokerage firm can lend you money, with those investments as collateral, for what is called a margin loan. If the value of your collateral investments drop down far enough, you'll get the usually dreaded margin call from your broker, and you'll have to pony up more securities or cash to meet the minimum requirements.

SELLING SHORT

When most investors buy stocks, they're hoping share prices will rise over time. This strategy is called buying long. Short selling, a daring investment strategy, takes the exact opposite approach: Short sellers are betting that the share price of the stock they just sold will decline, hopefully far and fast.

On top of that, selling short means selling shares that you don't already own: You sell them first, then plan to buy them when the price drops. In the middle is your broker, who loans you the shares to sell, and whom you pay back with the shares you buy. When you place the original order, you must be explicit: You're legally required to identify a short sale trade when you place the order. When you short a stock, you also must use a margin account. That account must be worth 150% of the value of the securities you're shorting. That 150% includes the short position.

Be Aware

If a stock you've borrowed pays a dividend, you will have to pay that dividend to the broker who loaned you the stock.

The biggest risk of short selling doesn't exist for buying long. This is because by selling short you can lose more than your original investment. If the stock price rises, you will take a loss. In fact, the loss potential is unlimited because there's no cap on how high the share price could climb. Regardless of the new share price, you're required to pay back every share you borrowed. For example, if you sold short shares at $20 per share, but the price rises to $50 per share, you would lose $30 per share. If you had bought those shares normally, hoping that the price would rise, and the price dropped to zero, you would only be out your $20 per share investment.

Why would anyone take that unlimited risk? Because with careful research and objective motivation, short selling can be a way to profit when a stock is losing ground.

SHORT STEPS

The flow of a short sale depends in part on how the specific stock actually performs. We'll start with an example of a successful short. For the example, we'll ignore margin interest and brokerage fees, both of which would eat into your profits (or magnify your losses) in a real trade.

First, you identify a stock, let's call it ABC Corp., and you think it will drop in price soon. Right now ABC is trading at $10 per share.

Next, you place a short sale order for 100 shares of ABC, a total of $1,000, with your broker. Before he'll execute the deal, the broker makes sure you have at least $500 in your margin account (50% of $1,000).

Your broker borrows those 100 shares of ABC Corp., sells them on the open market, and puts the $1,000 proceeds into your account.

A few days later, the ABC share price drops to $9 per share. You buy 100 shares at that price, and return them to your broker, for a $100 profit.

But if the stock price instead climbed to $12 per share, the story would go differently. If you decided to wait rather than buy the stock at $12, you would have to add another $100 to your margin account (50% of the $200 price difference). Let's say the stock stuck at $12 per share, and you decide to buy it to close out your short position so as not to potentially lose even more money. As a result, your overall loss would be $200.

ANNUAL REPORTS

An Investment in Knowledge

Most people would rather walk over hot coals than peruse the endless rows of numbers found in financial documents. Corporations understand that, and so they fill their annual reports with glossy color photos and colorful commentary. Corporations also know that a lot of people assume that a heavy, glossy report means a successful year. The numbers inside, though, may tell a completely different story. It's up to you to get comfortable with the numbers. When you do, you'll be able to look past the glossy pictures and discover the truth about a company's successes and failures.

If you're already a shareholder, you'll automatically get a copy of the annual report every year. If you haven't yet invested in the company, you can simply call and ask for one or look at it online. Every company's report looks different, and they may be assembled in different orders. However, every publicly traded company's annual report contains the same basic items:

- Letter from the chairman of the board (expect a big pile of spin here)
- A description of the company's products and services (more spin)
- Financial statements (read the footnotes carefully; they contain some of the meat)
- Management discussion (sort of a big picture look at the company, with a little spin)
- CPA opinion letter (read this to make sure the company's financial position is accurately represented)
- Company information (locations, officer names, and contact information)
- Historical stock data (including dividend history and dividend reinvestment plan program information)

GETTING THROUGH THE GLOSS

Don't judge a company's success by the look of its annual report. Stuffed with gorgeous full-color photos on heavy glossy pages, these reports aim to show the corporation in the best possible light. By focusing on positive results (no matter how insignificant) and possible future plans, a company can redirect investors' eyes away from troubling events and disappointing numbers.

With its professional presentation, the annual report highlights letters from the CEO and chairman who put their spin on the company's prospects as they describe the business. They fill the report with graphs and charts that look positive, but these graphics may not really say much when you look a little deeper.

So while the gloss may be more interesting to read, it's important for you to look at the numbers, too. After all, the numbers are of vital importance to investors, especially when it comes to the success or failure of the stocks they own or want to own.

FINANCIAL STATEMENTS

The financial statements in the annual report contain basically the same information as in the Form 10-K that the company filed with the SEC, but that information may be more abbreviated here. The three main statements you'll want to review are the:

1. Balance sheet
2. Income statement
3. Cash flow statement

The balance sheet gives you a snapshot of the corporation on the last day of the fiscal year. This report shows the company's assets, liabilities, and equity: what they own, what they owe, and their net worth. Assets are generally listed in order of liquidity, beginning with cash and ending with fixed assets (things like manufacturing plants and heavy equipment).

The income statement shows you the company's profitability over the year. It starts with revenues, then subtracts costs and expenses to get to the net profit or loss, the bottom line.

Profits Don't Mean Cash

Just because a company reports profits on its income statement doesn't mean that the company has cash. Profits and cash are not the same thing, and a company can have one without the other.

The third report all investors should review and understand is the cash flow statement. This report tracks how cash has moved in and out of the company during the year. Investors can use it to follow the cash trail. The report also tells you where the money came from, which is crucial information if you're considering buying the company's stock. Money that came from operations is what you want to see; it shows that the company is successfully selling its products and services and managing its costs and expenses. If the cash inflow instead comes from borrowing or issuing more stock, that could raise concerns about the profit potential of the company.

READ THE FOOTNOTES

There's a common saying among financial professionals: Accountants hide the problems in the footnotes. That's because financial statement footnotes are a lot like fine print: text that we all know we *should* read, but don't. The truth is, many (if not most) of us don't have the patience to get all the way through it. Corporations know that, and use it to their advantage.

That sounds shady, but it's not. In fact, it's perfectly legal. Moreover, it is extremely common for corporations to disclose important information in the footnotes to their financial statements. Even if a company has nothing to hide, these footnotes are where management can offer expanded insight into current operations and future plans—information investors need to know. While the financial statements contain all the numbers, the footnotes explain those numbers: how they were calculated, and where they came from, along with a deeper explanation of the results.

Why Recognition Time Matters

If you've ever shopped online, you know that some companies charge your credit card as soon as you click the "order" button, while others wait until your item has been shipped. Revenue recognition timing follows a similar principle. Some companies account for revenue when a product is ordered, others when a product is delivered. The distinction makes a difference for how they measure sales.

In the first section of footnotes, you'll usually find the details of the company's accounting practices, such as which valuation methods they've chosen to use and when they recognize revenue.

These choices reveal critical aspects of the corporation's earnings. To judge whether their choices make sense, you can find out what the standard is for that industry, and whether this company is following that standard. If it isn't, and this company is using a more aggressive accounting method, then it could be a warning sign that the company is trying to obscure negative performance or is using bookkeeping tricks to make their performance seem better than it is.

The next section of the footnotes usually spells out details and disclosures, information the company is required to provide that doesn't quite fit into the financial statements. Examples of information normally found here include details about:

- ESOPs (employee stock ownership plans)
- Outstanding stock options
- Long-term debt
- Ongoing or upcoming legal battles
- Error corrections
- Accounting adjustments
- Changes in accounting procedures

Keep in mind, like the fine print in credit card agreements, the language in financial statement footnotes can be full of legal jargon, making it even more difficult to wade through. Though it's not always the case, longer paragraphs and more challenging language are often used to hide what the corporation doesn't want the investors to read. For example, Enron disclosed a lot of their shenanigans in the footnotes of their financial statements, but virtually no one bothered to read them.

STOCK TABLES

All in a Row

Stock tables offer critical current information about stock prices. In order to monitor your stock investments accurately, it is vital that you become adept in understanding stock tables. Stock table information may vary slightly among different publications and websites, but the basic information is generally presented in a similar manner, with the stocks listed alphabetically.

There are a few things you should know about stock tables. For one, the date on a stock table is the date on which the trading activities occurred, not necessarily the date on which the information was published. Additionally, you will need to learn some stock table terminology, including the following:

- 52-wk high-low. This is usually the first column in a stock table. It shows the highest and lowest prices for which the stock was traded over the past fifty-two weeks.
- Company symbol. This column lists the ticker symbol (the abbreviated name) of the corporation that issued the stock.
- Dividends. This column notes the dividends the corporation pays to its shareholders.
- Volume (abbreviated VOL). This column tells you how many shares were traded that day, in multiples of 100.
- Yield (abbreviated YLD). This column estimates the dividend yield, which is calculated by dividing the dividend (as listed in the Dividends column) by the closing price (as listed in the Close column).

- Price-to-earnings (P/E) ratio. This column shows you the P/E ratio, which is calculated by dividing the share price by the corporation's earnings per share.
- High-low. This indicates the highest and lowest prices for which the stock traded that day.
- Close. This column indicates the last price at which the stock was traded during the day.
- Net change (abbreviated net chg). This column records the difference between the previous day's closing price and the current day's closing price, measured in dollars.

One thing that puzzles stock market newcomers: Why doesn't this morning's open always match yesterday's close? The open and close both reflect the price people are willing to pay for a particular stock, and a lot can change between 4:00 P.M. one day and 9:30 A.M. the next. The twenty-four-hour news cycle combined with an upsurge in after-hours trading can cause some pretty big differences between the two prices.

Most major Internet news sites post up-to-the-minute stock tables, and many of them are interactive so you can click through and see daily news information about a company or an industry. To get an instant quote for any company's stock, just type the ticker symbol into a search engine, and the most current information will appear. You should see the same basic data that appears in the full stock table, along with extra information, like market capitalization, three-month average volume, and historic pricing.

TICKER SYMBOLS

What's in a Nickname?

Stock or ticker symbols are the abbreviations used to represent a stock (and other types of investments like mutual funds and ETFs, or exchange-traded funds). The symbols are primarily used to help investors and traders keep track of and find information about a security. Whenever an investor uses a quoting service, he will need to enter in the ticker symbol in order to get the right data.

The company usually creates its own stock symbol, and the symbol typically represents the name of the corporation. For example, the ticker symbol for Microsoft is MSFT, and the ticker symbol for Archer Daniels Midland is ADM. However, not all symbols correlate directly with the name of the company they represent. For example, the stock symbol for Anheuser-Busch is BUD, and Harley-Davidson goes by HOG. It's important for investors to learn the correct symbol for each company they invest in and each company they're researching for potential investment; some symbols are quite similar, and it's critical to use the right one.

Ticker Trivia

Cedar Fair, L.P., is a publicly traded company with the seemingly unlikely stock symbol FUN. But the symbol is more appropriate than you'd think. Cedar Fair owns eleven amusement parks around the United States. You may have been to Dorney Park and Wildwater Kingdom (Pennsylvania), Kings Dominion (Virginia), or Knott's Berry Farm (California), all of which are owned and operated by Cedar Fair. No wonder their symbol is FUN!

EXTRA LETTERS

The number of letters in a company's ticker symbol lets you know on which exchange the stock trades. The NYSE uses stock symbols of up to three letters for their listed companies. Companies listed on the NASDAQ exchange use four letters, if the stock issued is common stock.

Sometimes, though, you'll see extra letters added on to a ticker symbol, and that can happen for a lot of different reasons. While most often those extra letters indicate some kind of problem with the shares, sometimes they simply designate a different share type.

A designation of "PR" following the ticker symbol indicates preferred stock on the NYSE. That PR may also be followed by another letter to designate the class of shares. For example, the ticker symbol for Bank of America preferred stock Series L trades as BAC.PRL. Corporations that offer multiple classes of common stock also have an extra letter tacked on their ticker symbols. For example, the two classes of Berkshire Hathaway stock trade as BRK.A and BRK.B.

Sometimes NASDAQ stocks have similar extra letters, denoting share class or preferred status. Other times, it's because the security being traded is not a common stock. When a stock trading on the NASDAQ has a fifth letter *added* to its ticker symbol, it's time to pay close attention, especially if that letter is E or Q. Each fifth letter has a specific meaning. The fifth letter codes are explained on the accompanying table.

CODE	MEANING	CODE	MEANING
A	Class A	N	3rd Class Preferred Shares
B	Class B	O	2nd Class Preferred Shares
C	Issuer Qualifications Exceptions	P	1st Class Preferred Shares
D	New Issue	Q	Bankruptcy Proceedings
E	Delinquent in Filings with the SEC	R	Rights
F	Foreign	S	Shares of Beneficial Interest
G	1st Convertible Bond	T	With warrants or with rights
H	2nd Convertible Bond	U	Units
I	3rd Convertible Bond	V	When issued and when distributed
J	Voting	W	Warrants
K	Nonvoting	X	Mutual Fund
L	Miscellaneous situations	Y	American Depository Receipt (ADR)
M	4th Class Preferred Shares	Z	Miscellaneous situations

Shares traded over-the-counter (OTC) typically have five letters, and shares traded on the pink sheets are always followed by "PK." Stocks trading on the OTCBB (Over-the-Counter Bulletin Board) will be followed with "OB." Online, these ticker symbols are preceded by a tier symbol (like a stop sign, for example). Ticker symbols on the over-the-counter exchanges are assigned by FINRA, and are not chosen by the companies.

CHANGING SYMBOLS

There are a few reasons a corporate ticker symbol might change. In some cases, the company initiates the change itself. Other times a symbol is altered by the exchange that the stock trades on, or it can be changed by a governing body like FINRA.

The two main reasons a company would change its own symbol are because of a name change or because it has merged with or been acquired by another company. In the case of a true merger, where a new company is formed, the two companies' ticker symbols will both change to reflect the new business. When a company is acquired, it may change its symbol to that of the acquiring company. For example, Walgreens originally traded as WAG—in fact, it used that symbol for almost ninety years. After it bought up Alliance Boots, merging with one of the largest European drugstore chains, the symbol changed to WBA.

When a company's ticker symbol is changed by an outside entity, it is usually an indication that something has gone wrong. For example, a company can be delisted, meaning it is no longer allowed to trade on one of the major exchanges. If that happens, it will trade only over the counter. In that situation, the old symbol will be tagged with "PK" or "OB." Companies that neglect to file financial statements and other required paperwork on time get a letter E added on to their symbols. Once they file the appropriate paperwork, that E can be removed by the governing body.

TICKER TAPE

This Has Nothing to Do with Parades

If you've ever watched a financial news show on TV and seen a line of cryptic letters and numbers scrolling across the bottom of the screen, you've seen what's known as the ticker tape. That information, properly decoded, helps investors and other market watchers stay on top of market trends and stock prices as they change throughout the trading day.

Originally recorded on tiny strips of paper, the ticker tape now appears in electronic format. But its function is still the same: to record every single transaction that takes place on the floor of the exchange. Ticker tape was first created in 1867, thanks to the introduction of telegraph machines. The latest price figures were delivered by runners who brought the tape from the market floor to the traders' offices. With this system, the brokerage houses closest to the trading floor got the news first, a distinct advantage.

By the 1960s, the tapes moved faster, but there was still a lag between the time the trade occurred and the time it was recorded. That delay was sometimes as long as twenty minutes, veritable centuries in today's world of instantaneous trading.

Ticker Trivia

A tick refers to any movement in the price of a security. Whether it goes up or down, whether the change is miniscule or notable, every move counts as a tick.

Finally, in the mid-1990s, a real-time ticker changed the pace of information. Electronically captured and broadcast, the data was put in everyone's hands at the same time, so the physical tape is no longer needed.

The ticker appearing on the bottom of the TV screen reports the trades of a single stock exchange. Some channels or programs will scroll two tickers across the screen to supply information from two exchanges, most commonly the NYSE and NASDAQ.

DECODING THE TICKER

The swiftly scrolling ticker tape seems puzzling at first glance. Once you know how to decode it, though, you will discover that it offers a wealth of up-to-the-minute information.

To break down a ticker tape, let's look at a bit of the strip:

TICKER SYMBOL	SHARES TRADED	PRICE TRADED	CHANGE DIRECTION	CHANGE AMOUNT
FB	25M @	119.41	Δ	1.12

First up is the ticker symbol, which identifies the company, in this case Facebook (FB).

Next is shares traded, which refers to the size of the trade being quoted, in this case 25 million. The letter M following the 25 stands for millions of shares; a K would mean thousands of shares, and a B would mean billions of shares. That's followed by @, showing that the shares traded *at* the price mentioned.

Price traded indicates the last bid price for the stock.

The fourth bit of information, change direction, lets you know whether the stock price rose or fell compared to the closing price on the previous trading day. Change amount lets you know how much the current price differed from the closing price on the previous trading day. In our example, it means the price of a share of FB is trading for $1.12 more than it did at the prior day's close.

Some tickers use different colors to let viewers see immediately which way a stock price is moving. Though there's some variation, most use green to show stocks trading higher, red to indicate stocks trading lower, and white to show stocks that haven't changed from the closing price on the previous trading day.

WHICH STOCKS MAKE THE TICKER?

With thousands of stocks and millions of shares trading every day, the ticker that rolls across the TV screen can't possibly include every single transaction. Only select quotes are displayed, and those are selected based on a few criteria: trading volume, how widely shares are held, price change, and breaking news. To get a spot on the ticker, a stock generally must be a big name or big news, and placement on the ticker varies minute to minute during trading hours. Stocks with high trading volume will show up more times than stocks with less trading volume, for example, and a company that's all over the news will get more play than a quietly trading corporation.

Once the exchanges have closed for the day, the ticker runs in alphabetical order and displays only the last quote of the day. The action resumes when the markets reopen the next morning.

INVESTOR MATH BASICS

Yes, You Have to Do Some Math

After you've narrowed your focus of potential stock purchases to a handful of companies, you should continue your research efforts by reviewing a few factors for each company. Find out about each company's earnings per share, price/earnings ratio, book value, price volatility, dividends, number of shares outstanding, and total return. These factors will give you greater insight into the stocks.

While some of the numbers (like earnings per share) can be pulled straight from a corporation's annual report, others may require a little math on your part (like price/book value ratio). Don't let the math stop you—it's all pretty straightforward and not terribly time-consuming. And the information you'll get from it is well worth the effort.

BOOK VALUE

Book value (which is also known as accounting value) shows a company's net worth, its equity. In a nutshell, book value tells you how much of the company is owned rather than owed. To calculate a company's book value per share, first subtract its total liabilities from its total assets (both of which you'll find on the balance sheet), and then divide that result by the number of shares of common stock outstanding.

Knowing this ratio can help you figure out whether the share price (the market value) makes sense as compared with the company's actual intrinsic value. Many experts say that a good way to find value stocks is to look for companies whose stock price is less than double their book value per share.

Visiting the Website

Corporate websites are an invaluable source of information in helping you make your investment decisions. In a study of individual investors, 74% said they visit a company's website before investing in a company, and 53.6% said they visit often before making a final decision to invest.

PROFIT MARGIN

When it comes to corporate profits, one of the most important pieces of information is the profit margin. This tells you what percentage of sales actually ends up as earnings. A company can have record-breaking revenues and meet every sales goal, but if they can't keep any of their earnings, what does that matter?

A company's profit margin is calculated by dividing its net income by its revenue. Generally speaking, higher profit margins are better, but like so many other factors, this one is relative. Looking at a single period's profit margin gives you a little information, but comparing it with other periods lets you see a pattern. For example, if a company has shown profit margins of 10% over the last five years except for one quarter where it shrank to 3%, that says something different than an average 10% profit margin that bounces around between 3% to 20% over the same period. The first example indicates steady, reliable profitability, which is a very desirable quality for a potential investment. The second example shows volatile and unpredictable profits, which don't bode well for the company's financial security. A pattern of consistently decreasing profit margin should throw up a red flag as this could indicate that the company is saddled with rising costs or is losing market share. In addition, it's helpful to compare the company's profit margin with its industry average. If it seems way out of whack, savvy investors will find out why.

PRICE VOLATILITY

Price volatility refers to how much the share price varies. It is usually calculated by looking at the difference between a stock's high and low prices over a set time period. This factor is important in determining the risk of a potential investment. You might not be as willing to pay a lot for a stock if you knew that its price had jumped up and down dramatically over the past few months.

In stocks, the term that describes price volatility is "beta." This is a quantitative measure of the variability when compared with the market as a whole. In most analysis, beta compares the changes in a stock's price against changes in the S&P 500 stock index. For example, a stock with a beta of 2 varies twice as much as the S&P 500. That stock can then be expected to rise in price by 40% if the S&P 500 rises by 20% or drop by 40% if the S&P 500 falls by 20%.

PAR, BOOK, AND MARKET VALUE

Three Numbers, Three Theories

There are a lot of numbers thrown around when people are talking about stocks. Some of those numbers matter a great deal, and some don't matter as much, at least not to investors. Among them are three different values: par, book, and market. Some people use these terms interchangeably, but they mean very different things.

PAR VALUE

The dollar amount actually listed on a stock's certificate is called par value. On common stock, this is usually a very small number, sometimes just a fraction of a cent. In fact, some stocks are issued with no par value. That's because par value is also redemption value, and a stockholder could redeem his shares for par value. For example, if par value was ten cents per share, and you had 10,000 shares of stock, you could legally redeem them for $1,000.00. If the company was floundering, and the market price actually dropped below the par value, the company would be on the hook if shareholders chose to redeem their stock (at least in theory). That's why it's very common for corporations to issue no-par common stock. Whether a corporation is allowed to issue no-par shares depends on the laws of its home state (where it was created rather than its base of operations).

While par value matters a lot from an accounting perspective, it doesn't have anything at all to do with stock price.

BOOK VALUE PER SHARE

In its most basic sense, the book value per share is the amount of money that would be doled out for each share of stock if a corporation had to fold. The calculation is based on the company's total equity, which works just like the equity in your home. To figure that out, you would take the value of your house and subtract the amount you owe on your mortgage. The result is the equity you have in your home, the amount of your house that you actually own.

It's the same for a corporation. To figure out the total equity, start with everything the company owns (its assets), then subtract everything the company owes (its liabilities). To figure out the book value per share, you take that total equity and divide it by the total number of common shares outstanding.

Sometimes, the calculation is not that straightforward. If the corporation has also issued preferred stock, for example, that claim would take priority over common stock shares, and would have to be added into the equation.

Book value per share is really a measure of the company's worth based on its balance sheet, which is a key financial statement that acts like a snapshot of the corporation at a specific moment in time.

MARKET VALUE

To an investor, market value is the most important of these three values because it reflects how the overall stock market feels about this company. It is literally the price you have to pay to buy shares.

While both earnings and earnings growth may be the most customary measures on which stock prices are based, several other factors come into play. Name recognition, for example, has a large impact on stock price because well-established household brands add value to a corporation simply through their existence. Well-respected and recognizable employees also can lead to increases in a company's stock price, as their inclusion gives investors confidence in the ongoing success of the corporation. Competitive barriers affect stock price as well, because they can hinder other companies from entering an industry. For example, exclusive contracts can give a company a distinct edge, and keep competitors from poaching locked-in customers or suppliers.

The total market value of a corporation can change rapidly. You calculate this by multiplying the current stock market price by the total numbers of shares outstanding. If Corporation ABC has 10 million shares outstanding, and the current stock price is $25, then the total market value of the company would be $250 million. When brokers or analysts are talking about the value of a corporation, this is what they mean.

EARNINGS PER SHARE

The Real Bottom Line

Earnings are the whole point of business, and every company aims to improve its bottom line. Without sustained positive earnings, a corporation cannot survive. As a potential stockholder and part-owner of a corporation, earnings are a crucial component to consider. In fact, for most investors, earnings is the number-one criteria by which to judge a company.

Earnings per share, usually abbreviated as EPS, lets you know how much of the company's total earnings (also called profits or net income) is earmarked for each individual share of the corporation's stock. The math to calculate EPS is pretty straightforward: It's the company's reported net income divided by the number of common shares outstanding.

How Many Shares Are Out There?

The number of common shares outstanding is not set in stone. That's because there are a number of different ways to arrive at that number. The number of shares could be based simply on how many shares of common stock are actually outstanding on the last day of the period. Alternately, it could be calculated as the weighted average number of shares that have been outstanding during the period, which could be different if shares were either issued or bought back by the corporation. Finally, the number could represent what's known as diluted shares, which is a much more complicated calculation that takes into account how many shares would be outstanding if every security that *could be* converted into common stock (such as stock options and convertible preferred shares) were converted.

To fully evaluate EPS and growth, though, it's important to know how the corporation has calculated its earnings, and whether their computation methodology has changed over time. Generally speaking, corporations have a lot of leeway when it comes to figuring their earnings, and it's to their advantage to show earnings in the best possible light to keep investors focused on what the company wants them to see.

WHAT "EARNINGS" REALLY MEANS

At the basic level, earnings are calculated by subtracting a company's costs and expenses from their revenues (sales). When a company uses its resources (assets) effectively and efficiently, those revenues will be higher than the costs and expenses. As a result, the company will have positive earnings. When the opposite holds true, and costs exceed revenues, the company suffers a loss, or negative earnings.

Calculating earnings can be a complex proposition, and sometimes even a convoluted one. In fact, by applying different tax and accounting principles, the same underlying numbers can result in different reported earnings.

HOW CORPORATIONS MANIPULATE EARNINGS

Depending on a corporation's end game, they can color their earnings any way they want, as long as it's legal—and you'd be surprised by how many seemingly shady accounting practices are perfectly legal as long as they're disclosed. With all that flexibility, a company can easily manipulate their earnings number, and even report a different number to the media than they do to the SEC or the IRS. Because of this, investors need to know exactly what they're looking at, and how the corporation came up with the numbers.

SEC filings, including the Form 10-Q and the Form 10-K, are expected to follow a set of strict standards known as GAAP (generally accepted accounting principles). Even within these rules, though, there's a degree of flexibility that allows companies to make reporting choices, and those choices can greatly affect the bottom line.

Mind the GAAP

GAAP, which stands for "generally accepted accounting principles," is a set of clear-cut rules and procedures that corporations are expected to use to put together their financial statements. These principles are designed to help investors better use and understand a company's financial position by calling for consistency and fairness in reporting.

In addition to manipulating the numbers themselves, corporations may also employ some sleight of hand when it comes to announcing their earnings, especially if they haven't hit analyst projections and expectations. For example, a company could announce their earnings after the market closes on a Friday afternoon—a practice referred to as "burying the report"—so that investors can't act immediately on an unfavorable earnings report and potentially force the stock price down. Another way that corporations hide numbers is to release them as a downplayed afterthought, following more positive highlighted information. For example, a corporation might slip a poor earnings number into a statement that's primarily focused on an upcoming development (like a new product launch).

Though corporations are required to disclose all of the pertinent information related to earnings, they don't have to make it easy for you to find. Often, the information they don't want investors to see or focus on appears only in the footnotes to the financial statements.

EARNINGS GROWTH

Once you've got a handle on EPS, you can determine a company's growth rate by looking at how its earnings per share have changed over the years. When you're looking to buy stock in a corporation, finding one with a pattern of strong, consistent earnings growth makes a lot of sense. You can see if the stock you're interested in fits the bill by analyzing the company's earnings per share results over the past several years. This analysis will let you see how and which way these results may have changed, and whether any growth is expected to continue.

In addition to the rate of change, you'll want to consider the pace of change. Slow but consistent growth can be indicative of a stable company in a low-growth industry. Fast and fluctuating change may indicate great future growth potential, or it could mean the spike in earnings was temporary or due to a single factor that may not be repeatable.

PRICE-TO-EARNINGS (P/E) RATIO

You Paid How Much for That?!

One of the most basic and often-used measures of a stock's value is the price-to-earnings ratio, or P/E ratio. Though the calculation itself is simple and straightforward, dividing the per-share stock price by the current earnings per share (EPS), this key piece of data provides a wealth of information. Most important, it tells you how much you'll be paying for one dollar of the corporation's current earnings. While it might seem like looking for the lowest P/E ratios would be the best move for investors, that's far from the case. On top of that, what's considered "low" is relative.

Reviewing a company's price-to-earnings (P/E) ratio is an integral part of any stock selection process. Since stock prices reflect investor demand, this ratio tells you the price investors are currently willing to pay in proportion to the company's earnings. For example, a P/E ratio of 20 means that investors are willing to pay twenty times more for a stock than that stock's related earnings per share. That information is important, but it's just the starting point.

For one thing, many different stocks can have the same P/E ratio despite vast differences in stock price and earnings. For instance, a stock that's trading for $30 per share and posts $1.50 earnings per share would have a P/E ratio of 20; but so would a stock that's trading for $60 with earnings of $3 per share, or a stock trading at $5 per share with earnings of $.25 per share.

Once you know the P/E ratio of a particular stock, you can look at the relationship of that stock's P/E ratio to others in the same class. In most instances, you can find a company's P/E ratio, and those of its peers, online (or in the newspaper). By comparing it with companies in the same category (for example, other mid-cap growth stocks) and in the same industry (for example, other technology companies), you can see how a particular corporation stacks up.

When you're investigating a particular stock, compare its P/E ratio with that of other companies in the same industry and that industry as a whole. Since every industry has its own unique qualities, you will want to find out what the average P/E is for that particular sector. If a company has an exceptionally high or low P/E compared to others in its industry, it's not necessarily a bad thing, but it is important to find out the reason why their ratio is off. For example, a low P/E ratio could indicate that the company's growth has been stagnant, that the company is burdened with excessive debt, or that the stock could simply be undervalued—making it a great buy for value investors. A company with a relatively high P/E ratio could be overpriced, or it could have dependable future earnings growth brought on by a recent expansion, acquisition, or new product line—making it a good choice for growth investors.

INDUSTRY AND SECTOR RATIOS VARY WIDELY

Context is crucial when you're evaluating stocks, and delving into P/E ratios is no different: They need to be seen in the context of their business peers.

Some industries have consistently lower P/E ratios than others. For example, classic industries that have been around for decades, even centuries, tend to have lower P/E ratios than new or up-and-coming industries. Stocks of utility companies, for example, virtually always come with much lower P/E ratios than technology stocks do.

It's also important to see how a company (or an industry) stacks up against the broader sector it belongs to. That information helps you determine whether a company might be an industry leader or laggard.

Consider these varied sectors and industries and their relative P/E ratios (information courtesy of Yahoo Finance, May 25, 2016):

SECTOR	P/E RATIO	INDUSTRY	P/E RATIO	COMPANY	P/E RATIO
Financial	15.80	Accident & Health Insurance	12.90	Aflac	11.45
Utilities	16.29	Gas Utilities	14.60	Northwest Natural Gas Co.	24.42
Healthcare	40.41	Biotechnology	165.80	Incyte Corporation	325.32
Technology	26.3	Wireless Communications	5.10	T-Mobile US, Inc.	28.67

You can see how widely P/E ratios can vary from sector to sector, and even within a sector or industry. But this additional knowledge adds to the full picture of the stock you're evaluating.

THE PEG RATIO

Back to the Future

Earnings per share (EPS) and the price-to-earnings (P/E) ratio measure what's happened in the corporation's past. That's important information to be sure, but as an investor, you care even more about what will happen next. The PEG ratio, or price-to-earnings growth, gives interested investors a glimpse into a company's potential for growth.

Let's start with how the PEG is calculated: Divide the P/E ratio by the annual EPS growth rate. This gives you an indication of the market's expectations of the company's future earnings. Like the P/E ratio, lower PEG ratios can indicate undervalued stock. Taken together with the P/E ratio, it gives a more complete picture of the stock's true value, and whether it deserves a place in your portfolio.

You can use the PEG to help compare stocks with different price and earnings pictures to see which makes more sense for your investment strategy. Let's say ABC Corp., an up-and-coming biotech company, has a P/E ratio of 200 and an earnings growth rate of 40%. Another stock you're intrigued by, XYZ Company, an established soda manufacturer, has a P/E ratio of 40 and a 10% earnings growth rate. While that 40% growth rate makes ABC Corp. look like the obvious winner, calculating the PEG may tell a different story. The PEG for ABC works out to 5 (200 ÷ 40). The PEG of XYZ works out to 4 (40 ÷ 10). Based on those results, the tried-and-true soda company has a better PEG ratio as compared to the biotech firm, because investors are paying less for expected future growth.

TOTAL RETURNS

Show Me the Money!

The calculations we looked at earlier are all used for investment selection. Total returns looks at a different side of investing: how well your stocks are performing for you.

Most investors in stocks tend to think about their gains and losses only in terms of share price changes. But savvy investors also think about another very important part of the picture: dividends. Although dividend yields may seem more important when you are looking for income, and price changes dominate the scene when you buy growth stocks, your total return on any stock investment is extremely important. Knowing a stock's total return indeed makes it possible for you to compare your investment with other stock investments, but it also makes it much easier for you to see how your stock measures up to other types of holdings, such as corporate bonds, treasuries, and mutual funds.

To figure out the total returns on a stock you own, first add the change in the stock price (or subtract it if the price has gone down) since the beginning of the year to the dividends you've earned over the past twelve months. Then divide that sum by the stock price at the beginning of the twelve-month period. For example, suppose you buy a stock at $45 per share and receive $1.50 in dividends for the next twelve-month period. At the end of the period, let's say that the stock is selling for $48 per share. Your calculations would look like this:

- Dividend: $1.50
- Price change: up $3.00 per share
- $1.50 + $3.00 per share = $4.50
- $4.50 ÷ $45.00 = 0.10

Your total return is a 10% increase.

But suppose, instead, that the price had dropped to $44 per share by the end of the period. Then your calculation would look like this:

- Dividend: $1.50
- Price change: down $1.00 per share
- $1.50 – $1.00 per share = $0.50
- $0.50 ÷ $45.00 = 0.011

Your total return is only a 1.1% increase.

Knowing your total returns on an investment will help you decide if that stock still deserves a place in your portfolio, but it's not the only number to consider. Looked at together with other factors, like earnings growth, and measured against the appropriate benchmark index, you can get a more complete picture of the security's real value.

FIVE CHARACTERISTICS OF GREAT COMPANIES

Kick the Tires, Check the Teeth

A lot of stock analysis focuses on numbers, most of them representing information from the past. But since buying stock represents investing in the future, it's important to get a real feel for a company's prospects by considering the following five traits:

- Sound business model. You want to single out a company that has a solid business plan and a good grasp of where it wants to be in the years ahead, and a plan to get there. A company with a clear focus has a better chance of reaching its goals and succeeding than a company that just rolls along without a concrete plan.

- Superior management. An experienced, innovative, and progressive management team has the best chance of leading a company into the future. Star managers have had a major impact on their prospective companies, and a company will often witness dramatic changes when a new management team comes on board. When key management leaves an organization, you will often see major changes in the way a company operates.

- Significant market share. When a majority of individuals rely upon the products and/or services of a designated company, odds are the company has good insight into consumer preferences. Industry market leaders usually have a well-thought-out vision. However, the company with the strongest performance doesn't always translate into the best stock to buy. Be careful and look more closely at markets that have a glut of competitors;

sometimes the second-best company makes the best stock investment.

- Competitive advantages. A company that is ahead of the pack will often be on top of cutting-edge trends and industry changes in areas like marketing and technology. You want to single out those companies that are—and are likely to stay—one step ahead of the competition.
- New developments. If a company places a high priority on research and development, it's likely to roll out successful introductions. If the product or service takes off, the stock price may very well follow.

THE BUFFETT APPROACH TO SUCCESS

Many individuals want to emulate the successful investors. And why not? Warren Buffett, for example, has earned his fame by investing in quality companies instead of relying on technical analysis strategies. Buffett believes that if you buy stock in quality companies, you have no reason to sell your investments unless there is a serious underlying problem behind a price dip. Buffett believes that investors should understand a company and its industry before making any investment decisions.

Although Buffett prefers to buy companies at prices below their potential, price is not the sole consideration in his stock selection process. Buying quality companies for the long haul is key. If one of your star companies suffers a dip in its stock price, Buffett says, it might be a good chance to pick up some additional shares.

INVESTOR PSYCHOLOGY

Taking Emotion Out of the Deal

It turns out that many individual investors often act irrationally when it comes to making their buy and sell decisions. For example, they might trade based on the popularity of a stock rather than its value or growth potential. This emotional trading usually leads to losses, yet these investors continue to make the same types of investment decisions. The relatively new field of behavioral finance examines these poor decision-making strategies and links them to market irregularities like crashes and bubbles.

Here's how behavioral finance tends to work. People jump to buy a stock because it's hot. That drives up the price, and more investors snap up shares. It makes no difference that the company has an unproven track record or is loaded with debt—all that matters in the heat of the trading moment is the excitement of owning this very popular stock. The number of investors who jump on that bandwagon alters the patterns and directions of the stock market—and not necessarily for the better.

The irony is that while many investors have no problem plowing their hard-earned money into portfolios stuffed with complicated creatures like biotech or nanotechnology stocks, these very same investors pause when given the opportunity to invest in a classic alternative investment like a hedge fund or a real estate trust.

AVOID THE HERD MENTALITY

When people first start investing, they often believe they'll make their investment decisions based purely on facts and research. But despite these good intentions they end up letting their emotions run the show. This can lead to investments that don't fit into the investor's plans and portfolios. For example, it's very tempting to follow the herd and buy what everyone else is buying. But when a bubble bursts, like the tech bubble did at the end of the 1990s, investors learned the hard way not to invest in a sector just because everyone else is doing it.

Ticker Trivia

You can't outperform the market if you buy the market. Bernard Baruch, an economic advisor to Woodrow Wilson and Franklin Roosevelt, was a firm believer in this principle of market investing, saying repeatedly, "Never follow the crowd." If you buy with the crowd, you will achieve the same results as everyone else, good or bad.

Following the crowd is a major part of behavioral finance, and many investment professionals now use the lessons learned from this area of study to inform their overall strategies. Traditional market analysis is founded on the idea that investors behave rationally and make their decisions only after carefully considering all available information. Behavioral finance adds a more human component to understanding the actions of investors by applying some basic principles of psychology.

KNOW YOURSELF

Understanding yourself is an integral component to mapping out an investment plan. What's right for you might be disastrous for another investor. Knowing your long-term goals and determining how much risk you can tolerate is critical when dealing with stocks because of their inherent volatility. Look back at your investor profile and let it guide you.

If you find at any point after you've invested that you simply cannot handle the market's mood swings, you may want to re-evaluate your strategy. Even though your investment plan is not set in stone, you should be fully aware of your reasons for changing your original strategy. Maintaining realistic expectations will keep beginning investors from growing frustrated, disappointed, and disillusioned. It's unrealistic to expect a 15% return on your investment if you aren't willing to take any risks. Understanding market volatility and your reactions to it can help you create the best portfolio.

Once you have developed a strategy you're comfortable with, don't second-guess yourself. Stick with the plan until it makes sense to reassess; don't let herd movements derail your strategy. No matter what your investing style, you have a good shot at success if you invest in high-quality companies you believe will—among other things—continue a track record of good financial execution and financial management.

INSIDE TRADERS

I Know Something You Don't Know

Insider trading is one of the most widely known issues covered by the SEC. Insider trading, or insider information, refers to buying and selling publicly traded securities based on confidential information that has not been released to the general public. Because such information is not available to everyone, those insiders have an unfair advantage. But not all insider trading is illegal.

When corporate insiders trade stock in their own companies, they're supposed to report those trades to the SEC. As long as they make the official report, the trades are perfectly legal. But skip that report, and now the trade is illegal.

It's not just company owners who can be charged with illegal insider trading, and the list of potential insiders includes more people than you'd think. Basically anyone who looks to profit off information that the general public isn't privy to is on this list, namely:

- Corporate officers, directors, executives, and employees
- Family members, friends, and business associates of the people just listed
- Lawyers, brokers, bankers, accountants, printers, and anyone else who might get to see corporate documents before they're released

Insider trading rules are very strict, but they do make exceptions for certain circumstances, such as a trade that was planned or executed for a reason (like a pre-existing agreement) other than one that was done simply to profit from not-yet released information.

But the history of the stock market includes many tales of notorious inside traders, unscrupulous men and women who profited vastly from privileged foreknowledge with no thought for the millions of investors they hurt. The stories of Ivan Boesky and Martha Stewart provide two choice examples.

IVAN BOESKY

Ivan Boesky landed on Wall Street in 1966, opened his own investment firm by 1975, and quickly made a name for himself trading companies that were ripe for takeover. He seemed to have an almost magical sense for identifying takeover targets before any offer was made, buying up stock in seemingly uninteresting companies. And when the takeover offer inevitably came, the share price would skyrocket and Boesky would rake in profits, his apparent clairvoyance paying off.

With his amazing insights, Boesky was able to cash in on some of the biggest takeover deals of the 1980s:

- Getty Oil by Texaco in 1984
- American Natural Resources by Coastal Corporation in 1985
- Union Carbide Corporation by GAF Corporation in 1985 and 1986
- Gulf Oil by Chevron in 1984
- Nabisco by R.J. Reynolds in 1985
- General Foods by Philip Morris in 1985

Riding high on his success and popularity, Boesky published a book called *Merger Mania* in 1985. Of course, Boesky didn't have ESP or even incredible good luck; he was a criminal. Avoiding the arduous work of studying companies and markets, Boesky took a highly unethical shortcut: He paid major investment bankers for inside tips on upcoming takeover deals.

Ticker Trivia

Said to be the inspiration for the *Wall Street* movie character Gordon Gekko, Boesky is quoted as saying, "Greed is all right, by the way. I want you to know that. I think greed is healthy. You can be greedy and still feel good about yourself." [From the commencement address at University of California, Berkeley, Haas School of Business, May 1986.]

In a move to save himself, one of those investment bankers ratted on Boesky. The SEC called him out for trading on inside information, and Boesky was charged with illegal stock manipulation in 1986. Always one to look for a deal, Boesky brokered a secret plea bargain with the SEC by giving up other names in the insider trading network. He ended up serving just under two years in prison, and paying a $100 million fine. He was also banned from working with securities ever again.

MARTHA STEWART

In one of the most disappointing insider trading scandals of all time, homemaking queen Martha Stewart was found guilty and sentenced to five months in prison and a $30,000 fine in 2004.

Stewart had a sizeable investment in a company called ImClone Systems Inc., a pharmaceutical player that had a new cancer drug, called Erbitux, in front of the U.S. Food and Drug Administration (FDA) for approval. Investors were excited about the prospects, and ImClone stock was doing well. Until a fateful day in 2001, that is, when the FDA rejected the drug. Most of ImClone's investors lost money when the market reacted to that negative news. But, as it turned out, some had sold right before the FDA announcement.

Martha Stewart was one of those early sellers, along with Samuel Waksal, the CEO of ImClone, who shared a broker with the home-making maven. The stock was flying high on expectations and trading at more than $50 per share when Stewart sold her nearly 4,000 shares on December 27, 2001, and raked in almost $250,000. On December 31, the very next trading day, the stock price dropped by 16%. Just a few short months later, the share price plummeted, trading at slightly more than $10.

When initially questioned, Stewart indicated that she'd been planning to sell, and even had an agreement in place. But that story quickly fell apart, and tales of her illegal trade hit the papers, forcing her to resign in disgrace from her role as CEO of Martha Stewart Living.

BARONS, TITANS, AND TYCOONS

How Unbridled Greed Built America

The roots of today's big traders go all the way back to the beginnings of the U.S. stock market, a time when investing resembled the Wild West and investors acted like gamblers more often than not. It was a time when great names were being made, names that still resonate today: Morgan, Carnegie, Rockefeller, Vanderbilt.

Among these big traders, billions of dollars were earned and lost. Some of these men came from money, others from poverty. Their insights and foresights helped paved the way for modern industry and trans-American transportation. Many of them had run-ins with the law, others with criminals, and several faced off against each other. Through their riveting tales, we can begin to see how the financial markets shaped the United States, and how these men shaped the markets.

J. P. MORGAN

Though today we think of J.P. Morgan as an investment bank, John Pierpont Morgan was one of the most famous tycoons ever to trade on Wall Street. Morgan invested in dozens of enterprises, from railroads to steel mills to Edison's electric company.

Born with a silver spoon in his mouth, Pierpont (as he liked to be called) began his financial career courtesy of his vastly wealthy father, a leader in the banking industry. And while his father arranged his first job with a solid New York bank, Morgan soon stood out as a brilliant—and ruthless—financial mind.

Having started in banking, Morgan truly understood investing. He used his knowledge, skill, and experience to take over the U.S. financial markets. When the Panic of 1873 hit the U.S. economy, Morgan didn't flinch; he emerged even richer, with his position in the world of finance solidified. His most famous investment was buying Carnegie Steel for $480 million in 1901. With that, Morgan created U.S. Steel, and his investment more than doubled in size within just ten years.

Despite tangles with antitrust laws, Congressional investigations, and his reputation as a callous robber baron, Morgan twice bailed out the U.S. government during financial panics. In fact, during the Panic of 1907, Morgan pledged his money (and convinced others to join him) to stabilize the U.S. banking system.

ANDREW CARNEGIE

Born to working class parents in Dunfermline, Scotland, Andrew Carnegie had none of the childhood advantages that blessed J.P. Morgan. But by the end of his life, Carnegie's wealth rivaled Morgan's. In fact, the two fortunes collided when Carnegie sold his flagship steel company to Morgan.

As he began his teenage years, Carnegie's family made the exhausting journey to the United States, settling in the small town of Allegheny, Pennsylvania. There, Andrew Carnegie got his first job, earning little more than one dollar a week in a cotton mill. But Carnegie's natural intelligence and motivation were quickly recognized, and he was soon promoted to office work. In this career, he caught the attention of a Pennsylvania Railroad executive, Thomas Scott, who hired Carnegie to be his personal secretary.

Under Scott's employ, Carnegie saved his money. And then he began to invest it. In fact, Scott told Carnegie about an upcoming sale of shares in a business called the Adams Express Company. Though he needed his mother, Margaret, to mortgage their family home to come up with the full $500 needed to buy ten shares, Carnegie made that very first investment, which began to pay off quickly with handsome dividends. Carnegie relished receiving dividends, earning money without toiling, and he quickly reinvested them to earn even more. As it turned out, Carnegie had an incredible talent for peering into the future and investing in what he saw ahead.

Golden Eggs

Rumor has it that upon receiving his first dividend check, Carnegie said, "Here's the goose that laid the golden eggs!"

While he was fully enmeshed in the business of the railroad, Andrew Carnegie became interested in other types of companies. For example, along with idea man Theodore Woodruff, Carnegie was instrumental in bringing the first sleeper cars to the railroad. By the time he was thirty years old, Carnegie held investments in several industries, including iron works and oil wells. He got involved with the Keystone Bridge Company, working to transform old wooden bridges into heavy-duty iron ones. And through all of these investments, Carnegie built himself an income that topped $50,000 a year, an astonishing feat during the Civil War era.

During that time, an Englishman named Henry Bessemer developed a process to transform large amounts of iron into steel. Whereas iron was tough but brittle, steel was durable and flexible, which made it easier to work with. When Andrew Carnegie learned of the Bessemer process, he poured money into the fledgling steel business, and he invested in a steel manufacturing plant right outside Pittsburgh. Carnegie expanded his holdings, and he built innovative new mills that would give him an enormous edge over his competitors. And by 1873, when the U.S. economy slumped, Carnegie bought his competitors' mills, modernized them, and continued to rake in profits.

One key secret to Carnegie's vast financial success was an idea called vertical combination (sometimes called vertical integration). For example, he bought majority shares in the iron mines necessary to steel manufacturing, as well as shares in the railroads needed to move his products. These stepping stones come together to form a full path, increasing overall efficiency and reducing costs for the core business.

A Generous Man

During his lifetime, Carnegie gave more than $350 million to charity, including the funding to build Carnegie Hall in New York City.

JOHN D. ROCKEFELLER

Known as the richest man in the world, John D. Rockefeller was notorious for his cutthroat business strategies, which included crushing his competition, then buying up all their assets.

In a divine twist of fate, Rockefeller was born to a poor family in Richford, New York. After dabbling in several industries, his interests turned to oil, and it was there that Rockefeller made his mark. Rockefeller turned the burgeoning oil industry on its head, profiting in ways no one had ever considered before, fueled by the big demand for kerosene (light bulbs had not yet been invented).

Kerosene comes from crude oil, converted during a largely wasteful refining process. Where everyone else in the industry saw waste, though, Rockefeller saw opportunity. He turned several crude oil by-products into moneymakers: selling petroleum jelly to medical companies, offering paraffin to candle makers, and even creating a market for other waste by calling it "paving materials."

All of these products, including the premium kerosene, needed to be moved throughout the country. In those days, shipping was done primarily by rail. And with railroads competing for his extensive business, Rockefeller was able to insist on discounted rates in the form of rebates. With those steep savings, he was able to greatly undercut his competition, offer reduced prices to his customers, and crush his competitors.

During that time, in 1870, at age twenty-six, Rockefeller founded his crowning achievement, Standard Oil. He quickly bought up other oil retailers, turning Standard Oil into a corporation of corporations until it was broken up by the government into thirty-four separate companies, some of which can be traced to companies still operating today.

And when demand for kerosene dropped off, replaced with calls for gasoline as the new automobile industry got underway, Rockefeller quickly adapted his refineries to produce the new fuel, never missing a beat.

Ticker Trivia

John D. Rockefeller was the world's first billionaire, having earned more wealth than any other American in history.

CORNELIUS VANDERBILT

Born into poverty just before the turn of the century in 1794, Cornelius Vanderbilt later would come to the markets with a vengeance, ruthlessly taking over companies and industries by employing strategies never before seen (though now they're old hat). Branded a robber baron, Vanderbilt monopolized two industries crucial to the fledgling American economy: ships and railroads.

His story begins during a time when the country was going through seismic changes, and new technologies were rapidly making their way to the forefront of the economy; it was the time of an industrial revolution. Vanderbilt had an uncanny knack for understanding which new industries had the most potential. And when he identified one, he jumped straight in.

When he was just eleven years old, in 1805, Vanderbilt dropped out of school to go work for his father, an uneducated ferry operator. Just a few years later, he took $100 and bought a sailboat, which he used to shuttle goods and people between Manhattan and his home city of Staten Island, recouping his initial investment in under a year. To keep his business afloat, young Vanderbilt began employing business tactics that would later become his hallmark: He offered often better service for a fraction of the price his rivals were charging. Before long, those competitors were forced to pay him to move, or go out of business themselves. Those moves seem obvious now, but before Vanderbilt, undercutting the competition was virtually unheard of.

Soon steamboats came along, and before the invention was a decade old, "Commodore" Vanderbilt learned how to pilot one. By the 1840s, he commanded more than 100 of the vessels, all known for their comfort, speed, and cheap prices.

Around that same time, Vanderbilt realized that railroads were the future of industry, and he plunked his money down as one of the first investors in railroad shares. But without the benefit of a transcontinental railroad—it hadn't yet been built—the shrewd entrepreneur shifted his attention to his shipping holdings, earning his first million. In 1864, having earned $30 million, seventy-year-old Vanderbilt bowed out of the shipping industry and returned his eagle eye focus to the railroads.

To outsiders, it may have seemed like he was just buying up stock in railroads. And he accumulated many, including the New York Central, Canada Southern, Michigan Central, and Michigan Southern (among others). But Vanderbilt had a visionary plan: He intended to connect a route from New York all the way through to Chicago. Then he could put his standard strategy into play, which was to provide excellent service at very low prices to drown out any competition, and then form a monopoly.

Vanderbilt's plan hit a snag when he faced steep competition for the Erie Railroad. As he quietly bought up shares in the railroad, hoping to corner the market unnoticed, longtime competitor and business foe Daniel Drew set out to derail him.

Ticker Trivia

Vanderbilt received a Congressional Medal of Honor for lending his largest ship to the Union forces to aid their pursuit of a Confederate warship.

From his inauspicious beginnings, Vanderbilt changed the direction of his life and became a self-made millionaire, leaving an estate worth an estimated $105 million when he died in 1877.

FAMOUS AND INFAMOUS INVESTORS

Whatever It Takes to Win

Over the span of centuries, the fortunes of the greatest investors have fascinated us, but their personal stories are often even more intriguing. Although these famed investors amassed great fortunes in the stock market, not all of them were able to hold onto that wealth.

From quirky misers to investing innovators, these men and women changed the shape of the stock market and the face of investing. Among these legends are millionaires, billionaires, and paupers. There was one man who nearly destroyed the Bank of England, and a wealthy woman known as the Witch of Wall Street. Each of these legendary investors greatly influenced the stock market we know today.

WARREN BUFFETT

$68.4 billion.

That's the estimated net worth of legendary investor Warren Buffett as of May 2016. And the lion's share of that immense wealth comes from his shares in Berkshire Hathaway, a company he took over in 1962; a company that started out as a mere textile manufacturer. That company has morphed into a multinational conglomerate, with extensive holdings in many disparate industries: from banking to food to private aviation.

Buffett made his first investment when he was just eleven years old, six shares of a company called Cities Service Preferred (he gave three of those shares to his sister). That he chose to put his money in the market is not so surprising, considering his father was a stockbroker, who immersed young Warren in the world of finance.

Nebraska, Buffett's home state, truly suffered during the Great Depression, and growing up in that time and place had a lifelong impact on him. Thrifty with his money, and always looking to earn more, Buffett worked on a paper route at age thirteen. And at age fourteen, he earned enough to file his first tax return.

Throughout his teen years, Buffett remained enterprising, selling magazines and stamps door to door, and still delivering newspapers. He also went into business for himself (along with a friend), accumulating $2,000 by age fifteen. His investments and personal savings continued to grow, and he was able to help pay his way through college.

Upon graduating from the University of Nebraska, Buffett applied to Harvard Business School, and was rejected.

That turned out to be serendipitous. While instead attending prestigious Columbia University in New York, Buffett had the good fortune to learn from one of the keenest investing minds in the country, Benjamin Graham. From Graham, young Buffett learned about the principles of value investing, and he absorbed a key message: Every company has an innate value that's separate from its prevailing share price. He came away with his signature strategy, buying shares in companies that were worth intrinsically more than their stock prices suggested, companies that were undervalued by the market.

Soon after completing his college education, he started the Buffett Partnership, which eventually evolved into today's Berkshire Hathaway, to employ his investment philosophy. In fact, his first enormously successful investment was in Berkshire Hathaway, then a successful

New England textile company, now one of the world's largest conglomerates. Today, Berkshire Hathaway acts as a holding company with many subsidiaries, including such well-known companies as:

- Heinz
- GEICO
- Dairy Queen
- See's Candies
- Fruit of the Loom
- Pampered Chef
- Orange Julius
- Brooks Sports

In addition to those subsidiaries, Berkshire Hathaway has holdings in many more companies (including corporate giants like American Express Company, General Electric, and Wal-Mart Stores). He is so successful that even jaded Wall Street insiders wait on tenterhooks to see what Warren Buffett will buy or sell next.

Giving It All Away

Like many ultra-successful investors, Buffett dedicated an enormous share of his wealth to charity, pledging to donate 99% of his Berkshire Hathaway shares over time, much of that going to the Bill & Melinda Gates Foundation.

BENJAMIN GRAHAM

Financial security was the driving force behind Benjamin Graham's success. Born from his family's struggles after his father died when

Benjamin was just nine years old, the now-renowned investor dedicated his professional life to financial stability.

His Wall Street career began in 1914, when Graham joined an investment firm with a job as a messenger. Within six short years, Graham became a partner in the firm. Soon after that, he struck out on his own.

Reputedly personally wiped out by the market crash of 1929, Graham's investment partnership weathered that storm and eventually restored its coffers. Until the doors were closed in 1956, Graham's company brought its clients 17% average annual returns.

A keen investment manager and respected financier, Graham devoted much of his career to educating others. He began lecturing at his alma mater, Columbia University, in 1926 and kept at that for thirty years. During that time, he published *The Intelligent Investor*, which still serves as must-read material for serious investors.

Graham established two key investing principles that served him and his students quite well:

1. Fundamental security analysis
2. Value investing

Graham put forth the idea that an investment, in order to be successful, must be worth more than its share price. That is, it must be a good value. He also believed strongly in analysis, and judged companies by their numbers: balance sheets, profit margins, debt loads, and cash flow, among other things.

At the time of his death in 1976, Graham left a legacy of guiding principles to help investors thoughtfully analyze every stock they buy.

GEORGE SOROS

Though famed hedge fund manager George Soros is best known—and most despised—for his role as a currency pirate, his actions affected financial markets all over the world, including the stock market. As a speculator, this investing titan places very big bets on which way he thinks the markets will move, a practice that brought him enormous gains and losses, and made him one of the richest investors ever. But he didn't start out that way.

Born in Budapest, Hungary, in 1930, Soros's early life was darkly colored by the horrors of World War II and its devastating aftermath. At the tender age of seventeen, Soros fled Hungary to escape Soviet occupation and the weight of communism, landing in England where he first became involved in the world of finance. When he moved to the United States in 1956, Soros dove headfirst into investment banking.

By 1973, he established Soros Fund Management, a hedge fund that would later evolve into the renowned Quantum Group of Funds, funds that achieved massive success. Under his aggressive, speculative investing style, the fund posted huge returns, said to have come to more than 30% a year for nearly thirty years, including two years of returns greater than 100% (literally more than doubling the funds' holdings).

What Exactly Is a Hedge Fund?

A hedge fund is a private investment partnership that uses aggressive and risky strategies in the hopes of scoring huge gains. Only wealthy accredited investors are allowed to participate in these funds, which can invest however they want to and in anything they want to as long as they keep investors informed.

Those unbelievable returns were a direct result of Soros's underlying investing philosophy, termed "reflexivity." The basic premise is this: Investors' behavior has a direct impact on market fundamentals, and it's their actions that create the booms and busts that Soros sees as opportunities.

His most famous, and most infamous, deal brought Soros a $1 billion gain in a single day, and nearly wiped out the Bank of England. It was September 1992, a time when the British pound was strong, and Soros decided to bet against it. He borrowed billions of pounds, which he proceeded to convert into German marks. When the British pound crumbled, Soros reconverted those German marks at the new much more favorable exchange rate, and was able to repay his debt based on that new lower value of the pound. The difference between the values of the mark and the pound on that fateful day of September 16, 1992, brought George Soros more than $1 billion profit.

After that, Soros was feared by governments around the world, terrified that the ruthless speculator would fix on their currencies, and then bankrupt them. They were right: In 1997, he placed a similar bet on the Thai baht, and again prevailed. But not every gamble brought a win.

In addition to his currency killings, Soros invested heavily in the stock market. When he turned his attentions to a corporation, he bet big and fast, choosing stocks based on an ever-shifting combination of information and intuition. Sometimes his gambles paid off, other times he was faced with staggering losses. For example, Soros bet on the U.S. stock market in 1987, and lost close to $300 million when it crashed.

Ticker Trivia

According to George Soros, "If investing is entertaining, if you're having fun, you're probably not making any money. Good investing is boring."

Later in life, Soros turned his attention toward political activism and his vast fortune toward charity, creating the Open Society Foundation to forward his philanthropy. Through the foundation, George Soros has donated billions of dollars to causes all around the world.

THE WITCH OF WALL STREET

The life of Henrietta Howland Robinson Green, best known as Hetty Green, was drenched in rumor and scandal. Her odd nature and unusual dress—she almost always wore black, and wore her clothes until they became threadbare—led people to call her the Witch of Wall Street. But the combination of her keen investment insights and miserly habits (which earned her another derogatory nickname, Hetty the Hoarder) made Hetty Green one of the richest women who ever lived.

Born to a sickly heiress and a distant, merciless businessman in 1834, Hetty had a remarkable grasp of finance at a very young age. By age eight, she had already opened her own savings account. As a child, she read the financial section of the newspaper almost every day to her grandfather (he was virtually blind), all the while discussing investments in great detail. That education served Hetty in her role as bookkeeper for her father's business, which did nothing to ease their cold relationship. In fact, when her mother died, Hetty's father blocked her inheritance, forcing the young woman to wait for his passing. When he died in 1864, Hetty finally had access to her family legacy of more than $5 million.

A short time later, Hetty's rich aunt died. Hetty had been expecting another inheritance; she claimed that her aunt had promised to leave Hetty her fortune. When the will was read, though, Hetty received a miniscule portion of the estate, with the rest parceled out among doctors and caretakers, even some distant cousins. Hetty contested that will, and produced another. Extensive legal battles ensued, and accusations of forgery were tossed around. The particular judge that she blamed for these legal troubles didn't bank on Hetty's powerful vindictiveness. As soon as she was able, she used her considerable financial resources to have him removed from the Chicago district court. Eventually, Hetty was awarded $600,000 of her aunt's $2 million estate.

Not content with her current fortune, Hetty brought her new influx of cash to Wall Street, snapping up low-risk investments. When the market declined amid panic selloffs, Hetty bought in, buying at rock-bottom prices. Panicked bankers would come to her for emergency loans, which she gave them, as long as they agreed to her high-interest terms. As soon as the market turned around, she would demand immediate repayment with interest, and unload her cheaply bought investments for huge gains.

During the Panic of 1907, the Witch of Wall Street made the move that cemented her fortune. Her keen investor's intuition told her the market was heavily overvalued, prompting her to sell the majority of her holdings and call in all outstanding loans. She was right. While bankers and investors desperately tried to claw their way out of the gaping market bottom brought on by that great panic, Hetty Green quietly sat with her now-liquid fortune. When the dust settled, she bought up bargain stocks left and right. She now also required physical collateral (like land) for new loans she made. Though some painted her as a vulture, Hetty helped keep New York City solvent during that Panic, as their lender of last resort.

On the other side of the Hetty Green equation stood her near-pathological frugality. Despite her vast riches, Hetty moved around frequently, from one small apartment to the next, to get out of paying district taxes. One of the most heartbreaking examples of her miserly ways cost Ned, her only son, his leg. When the boy injured his leg, she brought him to a charity hospital to take advantage of their free care. His wound wasn't treated properly and became gangrenous, eventually leading to amputation, and replacement with a cork leg.

When finally she died in 1916, Hetty Green left a $100 million liquid legacy, allegedly accompanied by even more wealth left in holdings that did not bear her name.

CARL ICAHN

Hostile takeover king Carl Icahn had a knack for making corporate executives tremble in fear once he set his sights on their companies. But he didn't start out as a corporate raider.

Carl Icahn grew up in a middle class family in Queens, New York. He went to Princeton on scholarship, dabbling in philosophy and medicine (until he realized that he hated working with corpses). In 1961, he got an entry-level job as a stockbroker, and quickly outgrew it. By 1968, Icahn had bought his own seat on the NYSE. And by the late 1970s, he kicked off his career as a corporate raider.

His most dubious claim to fame: Carl Icahn inspired the creation of more new SEC regulations than any other person in history, particularly in the area of disclosure rules. One of the original corporate raiders, Icahn cemented his position in Wall Street lore by hijacking TWA in a hostile takeover.

Ticker Trivia

The "Icahn Lift" sends a stock price soaring when the takeover king buys up shares in a company.

A financial bulldog, Icahn is known for scooping up majority positions in corporations, and then forcing the management to make profound changes designed to increase the stock price.

The ultimate corporate raider, Icahn continues to take over unwary corporations, and wield enormous financial clout.

JESSE LIVERMORE

Jesse Livermore lived a true "rags to riches" story, though one that ended in overwhelming tragedy. Born in the town of South Acton, Massachusetts, in 1877, Livermore headed to Boston in his early teens, hoping to avoid a life as a farmer. It was there he first discovered stock trading. A natural risk-taker, Livermore made a fortune shorting stocks, making money while everyone else was losing. At the peak of his wealth in 1929, he was worth nearly $100 million. In between, he made and lost several fortunes. Torn by the financial ups and downs, he took his own life in 1940.

Before his ill-fated death, though, Livermore was one of the most celebrated investors of his time. With no financial background, experience, or education, Jesse Livermore learned from his own market wins and losses. His career began when he was just a teenager, working in Boston as a chalk boy for Paine Webber, posting stock prices in the office.

Ticker Trivia

Livermore's book *How to Trade in Stocks*, published in 1940, is still considered a must-read for serious investors.

Livermore dove headfirst into the stock market, raking in big money by the time he was fifteen: Rumor has it that he earned more than $1,000 in gains that year, a fortune in those days. Livermore earned a lot of his wealth by wagering against bucket shops, where all the action was based on stock price movements rather than stock trades. He was so successful that the Boston shops eventually banned him, spurring his move to New York City.

Decades before a click of the mouse brought up detailed price charts, graphs, and market news, Livermore's system involved gathering up available information and keeping track of stock prices and patterns in a handwritten ledger. His key strategy was to buy and sell stocks that were on the move. Once his stock target was selected, he watched for pivotal price points so as to carefully time his trades.

With his speculative style and focus on market directions, Livermore enjoyed staggering wins and demoralizing losses, and investors around the world eagerly anticipated his next moves.

DAVID DREMAN

Canadian David Dreman may not spark the same recognition as some of these other famed investors, but he perfected an investment strategy that has been followed successfully by many others: contrarian investing.

After losing a shocking amount of money in the late 1960s, and watching his wealth plummet by nearly 75%, Dreman learned the hard way that following the investing crowd was a surefire way to get burned. With that demoralizing experience behind him, Dreman began to look at the market in a whole new way, through the lens of investor psychology. That inspired his new contrarian investment philosophy, which boils down to "do the opposite."

Essentially, Dreman began investing against prevailing market trends and crowd behavior. He believed that herd behavior skewed stock prices, leading to mispriced shares. If he could exploit that difference then he could profit. In practice, he bought poorly performing stocks, and sold stocks that were doing well. Unlike mainstream investors, Dreman would seek out-of-favor corporations, focusing on those with low price-to-earnings ratios, then watch them outperform the market over time. And by the late 1970s, he had turned his fortune around completely, setting a remarkable example for novice investors.

THOMAS ROWE PRICE JR.

Contrary to the prevailing wisdom of his time, the dismal days following the Crash of 1929, Thomas Rowe Price Jr. didn't believe in jumping in and out of the stock market, following trends and cycles, and carefully timing stock purchases and sales. Instead, he looked for solid companies, corporations that he expected big things from in the future. Not surprisingly, with that aim in mind, Price was dubbed the "father of growth investing."

Despite growing up during the Depression, and beginning his career in the shadow of the Crash of 1929, Price tackled the stock market head-on, but in a manner very different than that of his contemporaries. Price studied companies, researched them, and bought for the long haul, an unpopular philosophy at the time. Dubbed "iron-willed" and tough to work with, Price's views were met with stony resistance from his bosses at the Baltimore firm Mackubin, Goodrich & Co. When the company decided to get rid of his department, Price left.

In 1937, Price struck out on his own, founding Price Associates, which has evolved into T. Rowe Price & Associates. He continued to work in his own distinct style, one we take for granted today but that didn't really exist before Price introduced it. Namely, he insisted on putting his clients' interests ahead of his firm's. To demonstrate his commitment, Price challenged the usual practices and set a new standard by charging client fees based on their holdings, and not charging commissions. In another landmark move, Price offered investment advice and counseling to his clients, something virtually unheard of at the time.

At the same time, he was fine-tuning his stock-picking methodology, focusing on the qualities he believed indicated superior long-term potential. Before investing in a corporation's stock, for example, an analyst from Price's company would meet with and interview the corporation's president. With his innovative system perfected, Price launched his company's first mutual fund, the T. Rowe Price Growth Stock Fund, back in 1950.

Still Growing Strong

The T. Rowe Price Growth Stock Fund still exists today, bringing investors average annual returns of nearly 11% per year since it launched sixty-six years ago.

After decades of helping investors build their wealth, Price retired in the 1960s, and then sold off his interests in the firm that still bears his name.

JOHN TEMPLETON

Though his life began humbly in Winchester, Tennessee, John Templeton ended his days a billionaire. Born to a poor family in 1912,

Templeton drove himself hard to succeed. He earned a scholarship to Yale, earning a degree in economics, and went on to earn a master's degree from Oxford University in England.

Just a few years later, in the midst of the Great Depression, the motivated young man (with a few partners) began an investment firm, which became enormously successful over the years, eventually growing into a $300 million business.

His dogged strategy, which he called bargain hunting, contributed to his wild success. In a classic, famous move, Templeton bought a $100 stake in every company whose stock was trading for less than $1. His investments in those 104 companies, some of which were actually bankrupt, roughly quadrupled in value in just four years' time. And he followed that strategy going forward, seeking out inexpensive companies of value that no one else was even looking at.

In 1954, Templeton launched the Templeton Growth Fund, his first mutual fund (a mutual fund is a big pool of money paid into by loads of investors so they can invest in a large, diverse portfolio of securities). Throughout his career, he established some of the most successful mutual funds in the world. In fact, his Templeton Growth Fund had astounding average annual returns of 13.8% over a fifty-year period.

JAMES "JUBILEE JIM" FISK

Jubilee Jim Fisk was murdered in a posh Manhattan hotel room in January 1872. The infamously unethical businessman had been involved in a scandalous love affair with actress Josie Mansfield, and the couple's notoriety saw them splashed all over the front pages. When the showgirl got together with frustrated businessman

Edward Stokes to blackmail Fisk, Jubilee Jim resisted, and Stokes ended Fisk's life with a bullet. As huge as the man himself, Fisk's funeral involved a state militia unit and a 200-piece band.

Fisk's life was as scandalous and storied as his death. He was born in Bennington, Vermont, in 1835, but young Jim quickly moved on to splashier surroundings. His early work involved stints as a waiter, a salesman, a peddler, a smuggler, and a circus performer. Eventually, Fisk became a stockbroker, and that is where his path collided with the much-despised robber baron Jay Gould. Once the money started rolling in, Jubilee Jim loved to throw it around, and he spent quite a bit of it on the New York nightlife scene. Among other interests, Fisk bought the Grand Opera House and several other theaters in the city.

Easily recognizable with his heavy build and handlebar mustache, Fisk was well known for his unscrupulous Wall Street business tactics, and he was intimately involved in schemes that caused financial panics and wild market swings. At times, Fisk partnered up with notorious robber barons to make his cutthroat moves. But most often his partner was the secretive, surly Jay Gould.

JASON "JAY" GOULD

Being declared the most hated man in America did not bother Jason "Jay" Gould in the slightest. In fact, he thrived on the animosity, scorning his detractors. He made his Wall Street mark through manipulation, piracy, bribery, blackmail, and strikebreaking. The unsavory Gould prided himself on purposely running businesses into the ground, then rebuilding them for his own benefit.

Gould was a sickly child, born to an impoverished family in rural upstate New York in 1836. Not suited for farming, he turned to other trades, working as a blacksmith, a tanner, a surveyor, and a leather merchant before he finally became a stockbroker. In this capacity, the railroad industry caught his eye, and it led to one of the most infamous stock market wars in American history.

When he and Cornelius Vanderbilt battled over control of the Erie Railroad in 1867, Gould pulled every dirty trick he could muster. As Vanderbilt continued to secure shares in the company, Gould (along with Jim Fisk and Daniel Drew) illegally issued more than $5 million in new stock, watering down Vanderbilt's holdings. In an attempt to avoid arrest, Gould snuck out of New York and into New Jersey, where he quickly set up a new headquarters. To keep the industrious Vanderbilt out of his financial records (Vanderbilt had reportedly sent goons to grab them), Gould set three cannons along the Jersey City waterfront and launched a mini-fleet of small boats stocked with armed men into the water. When the law caught up with Gould, he had the law changed by bribing New York legislators in Albany, making his once-illegal stock issue perfectly legal. In the end, Vanderbilt admitted defeat, leaving the Erie Railroad in the hands of Gould, Fisk, and Drew.

But the scintillating story of the Erie Railroad doesn't end there. Fisk and Gould forced Drew out of the railroad. A short time later, Fisk was murdered by his ex-girlfriend's new lover. That left Gould with their full shares of the Erie, until he was out-swindled by a man known as Lord Gordon-Gordon. Gould, in all his greed, wanted full control of the Erie Railroad, so he started to pull together cash and investors in order to buy up every share he could. Enter Gordon-Gordon, a Scottish "investor," who ensnared Gould in an elaborate web of lies. Gordon-Gordon convinced Gould that he could bring in even more aristocratic investors, and Gould responded by gifting the "lord" with nearly $1 million in Erie Railroad stock, which he turned around and sold immediately, funding his escape to Canada.

By 1879, Gould no longer had a stake in the Erie. Instead, he headed west, and set his sights on other growing railroads, including the Union Pacific.

Unlike many other affluent businessmen of his time, Gould never gave a dime of his vast fortune to charity. Despite his well-deserved reputation as a ruthless robber baron, Gould actually had some very positive effects on American society. Among those accomplishments, Gould was instrumental in forging a national railroad, as well as bringing Western Union to the top of the telegraph industry.

HISTORY'S BIGGEST SCAMS

Unleashing Tsunamis on Wall Street

Insider trading is one of the most widely known problems policed by the SEC, but it's not the only way investors can be scammed by corporations or their employees. While the SEC and reputable, honest public accounting firms work tirelessly to uncover frauds, a lot of schemes slip through, bilking shareholders out of millions—even billions—of dollars. And though corporate scams make for splashy headlines, a good story does nothing to help investors recoup their losses.

ENRON

Before the bottom dropped out in 2001, Enron, then trading at about $90 per share, was one of the largest and most successful corporations in the United States. At least that's what we were led to believe.

With an elaborate and complicated accounting scheme that kept hundreds of millions of dollars in debt off their financial statements, the company fooled investors and regulators alike, leading them to believe the company was much more stable than it turned out to be.

On top of that balance sheet deception, Enron executives fiddled with their revenues as well. They created shell companies, and used them to grossly inflate earnings figures. In addition, the company's auditors, prominent public accounting firm Arthur Andersen, never reported a problem. At best, these auditors were neglectful and incompetent.

Enron declared bankruptcy in December 2001, leaving thousands of employees jobless, and costing stunned investors dearly.

When their fraud was out in the open, the Enron stock price plunged to less than fifty cents a share.

Everyone from corporate officers to the CPAs were indicted on criminal charges. Some were sentenced to jail time, some died, and some saw their charges dropped. As for the company itself, Enron limped through that 2001 bankruptcy by selling off assets, including valuable pipelines. By 2006, the last asset had been sold off, and the company was re-formed and renamed Enron Creditors Recovery Corporation, now dedicated to paying off all the creditors caught up in the swindle.

WORLDCOM

Another fraudulent bookkeeping scandal, this one involving billions of investor dollars, followed right on the heels of the Enron scandal. WorldCom, a leading telecommunications corporation, engaged in some very creative accounting that greatly overstated their profits.

In this case, the company recorded normal business expenses (things like office supplies) as assets. Instead of deducting those expenses right away, they spread the costs out over several years. In fact, they capitalized nearly $4 billion of those normal operating expenses. And that deceptive accounting resulted in more than $1 billion profit, when in truth WorldCom really lost billions of dollars.

Again, employees were hit hard when the scam was exposed. More than 10,000 people lost their jobs. And shareholders didn't fare much better. They watched the stock price tumble from highs topping $60 per share to less than twenty cents per share.

In July 2002, the company filed the largest bankruptcy in history (as of then), with plans to reorganize under the name MCI.

As part of that deal, the corporation paid $750 million to the SEC (through a combination of cash and stock), intended to be distributed among the defrauded investors. Worldcom founder and CEO Bernard Ebbers is still serving out his 25-year prison sentence. And MCI was bought and subsumed by Verizon in 2006—a final end to the Worldcom saga.

BERNARD MADOFF

By the time he was arrested, in 2008, Bernard Madoff had committed the single biggest fraud in the history of the U.S. stock market: a $64.8 billion investment scam that duped thousands of sophisticated and institutional investors right along with SEC authorities. Though it's often said Madoff conned his investors out of $50 or $60 billion of losses, that's not exactly accurate. Rather, they lost their original investments, totaling about $20 billion; the rest never really existed.

When he first hit the stock market, though, Madoff dealt mainly in penny stocks on the over-the-counter (OTC) markets, acting as a market maker in the 1960s. In those early days, he took most of his earnings from the bid/ask spread on those thinly traded securities. As his investment firm grew, he began trading Big Board securities, and his company thrived. Around this time, Madoff began cultivating relationships with industry regulators, and that's where things begin to get interesting.

Intrigued by new emerging technologies, Madoff focused on automated trading systems, even creating one of the first computerized programs to match buyers and sellers, vastly improving trade efficiency at his firm. In fact, some industry insiders believe that Madoff's business was successful enough to bring in an estimated $25 million per year during the 1980s.

By the early 1990s, Madoff had become a financial industry staple, even serving as head of the technologically oriented NASDAQ stock exchange for three years. Madoff's advice was sought after and trusted, and big-money investors flocked to his investment fund, ignoring what should have been bright red flags because of their faith in him. And he didn't accept just any investor; he actually turned many would-be investors away, which only made his fund seem more exclusive and attractive.

A Parade of Familiar Names

The Bernard Madoff story might not have caught fire as quickly if it hadn't been for some very high-profile and popular names taken in by Madoff's scheming. Counted among the swindled investors were Hollywood icon Steven Spielberg, ubiquitous film and TV star Kevin Bacon, and infamous former New York governor Eliot Spitzer.

The money seemed too good to be true, and it was: Madoff's firm offered investors steady high returns from low-risk investments, the holy grail of investing because it's virtually impossible. But every year, investors were seeing returns in the neighborhood of 10% to 13%, and those earnings held steady even as the markets swung up and down. Madoff worked under a cloak of secrecy, often denying investors online access to their accounts, and clearing all of his own trades without oversight. And because of his close connections to SEC officials, no one looked into Madoff's firm until it was too late.

As it turned out, Madoff's investing genius was no more than a Ponzi scheme. Those high, reliable returns weren't real; they were simply funds from new investors paid out to those who'd bought in earlier. When it all collapsed, his investors were left with nothing. And though on June 29, 2009, Madoff was sentenced to 150 years in prison, that's of little solace to investors who lost everything.

Seven Years Later

In May 2016, the special master of the Madoff Victim Fund, Richard Breeden, announced that his office had finally completed the initial review process for more than $67 billion in claims. Breeden said he planned to recommend $4 billion in payouts to 25,280 victims of Bernard Madoff's fraud by the end of August 2016.

COMMON SCHEMES

Psst, Buddy, Wanna Buy a Solid Gold Watch for $50?

Creating false information about stocks is extremely easy to do. Virtually anyone with a laptop or a smartphone can create realistic-looking websites and press releases with just a few mouse clicks and judicious copy-and-paste action. Cold calling schemes are rampant, and new twists appear faster than ever before. Unsuspecting investors get caught up in the hype and excitement generated by hucksters. But investors who know the tricks of this illegal trade can avoid getting sucked into these schemes.

BOILER ROOMS

When it comes to high-pressure sales tactics, the infamous "boiler rooms" dominate. Set up in large, cheap offices, crowds of telemarketers randomly cold call potential investors to bully them into buying specific stocks. These stock pushers work for commissions, and they work aggressively, hawking otherwise unheard of companies with exaggerated and outright false information about skyrocketing sales, 1000% returns, and other outrageous claims.

Most often, the shares they're selling trade on the pink sheets, where there are virtually no disclosure requirements, and very little regulation. That Wild West atmosphere suits their purposes perfectly, as many of these "advisors" have no financial or securities qualifications at all. What they do have are persuasive personalities and intimidation tactics, and a very strong grasp on emotional manipulation.

PUMP AND DUMP

Unscrupulous brokers often hype and promote companies they hold shares in, even though those companies have only minimal assets and not a lot of prospects for real success. These ruthless salesmen contact potential investors by phone and e-mail, and post enticing messages on Internet bulletin boards, inflating the real value of the company and tagging it as "the next big thing."

With these pump and dump schemes, hard-selling wheeler-dealer brokers hype the stocks to thousands of people, making outrageous claims about the company that are wholly unsubstantiated by the facts. The companies they choose are typically micro caps, for which independent or verifiable information can be very hard to find.

With their high-pressure sales tactics, these brokers encourage investors to dive in, which sharply increases the trading volume and liquidity of the shares, and drives up the share price—the "pump." When the share price spikes, these brokers sell their shares—the "dump"—and cash in on that artificial price inflation, raking in profits for a company that is worth nearly nothing.

SHORT AND DISTORT

In bear markets, pump and dump schemes don't work all that well because investors are more wary. In times like those, a sort of opposite scheme goes into play: the short and distort scheme. Here, dishonest traders use short selling in an underhanded way to take advantage of naive investors.

This type of scam also involves stock price manipulation, but in the opposite direction. The traders bad-mouth their target stock, one for which they hold a short position, to drive down its price as far as possible.

These con artists play on investor fear and worry, already heightened by the bear market. For this scheme to work, they must appear trustworthy, and so they often pretend to be associated with trusted authorities like the SEC and FINRA. This is especially easy to do by e-mail. They claim to be looking after the best interest of the investor, protecting them from the "corporate liars" who are directly tied to the company. They try to convince investors to sell their shares because the company can't be trusted or some scandal is about to break. They may even mention class action lawsuits (that don't really exist), all in an effort to get investors to sell and force the stock price to bottom out.

When it does, they swoop in and buy up the shares at ridiculously low prices, shares that they have shorted at much higher, true value prices.

POOP AND SCOOP

Another twist on the pump and dump scheme is known as the poop and scoop, which mixes elements of the classic pump and dump scam and its short and distort cousin.

As with its fraudulent relatives, the poop and scoop scheme is highly illegal. The anonymity of the Internet makes this dastardly practice deadly easy to spread, and also very hard to trace.

To conduct this scam, a small group of investors (sometimes just one) try to send a stock price into a free fall by circulating negative false information about the corporation and spurring the rumor mill. All of that damaging publicity takes a heavy toll on the company's stock price, sparking a mad selloff.

Unlike the short and distort scam, the architects of the poop and scoop then buy up that stock at bargain basement prices. When the stock rebounds to its true value, these scammers sell, amassing large profits.

WRONG NUMBER

A new variation on the pump and dump scam is the "wrong number." For this scheme, con artists leave messages on your voicemail, pretending to be calling someone else with a hot stock tip.

These messages are very carefully crafted to make you think they were left by accident. In them, the caller recounts details of a smoking hot stock tip. And, believe it or not, many people fall for this scam, increasing trading volume and inflating share prices. When the price spikes, the "callers" cash out, leaving their victims with heavy losses.

PONZI SCHEME

Ponzi schemes made the headlines again during the Bernard Madoff scandal, in what was one of the biggest and mostly costly scams in financial history.

The first well-known scheme of this kind was perpetrated by an Italian immigrant named Charles Ponzi back in the 1920s. After being involved in a few unsuccessful criminal ventures, Ponzi came upon the scam of his life. He got a letter from Spain that contained an international reply coupon (IRC), a special coupon that let the holder trade it in for a specific number of priority postage stamps in another country. Ponzi quickly figured out that he could profit by having people abroad buy low-cost IRCs, have the IRCs sent to him, exchange them for more expensive stamps in the United States, and then sell the stamps. Allegedly, on some of these stamp sales Ponzi earned returns of more than 400%.

Then Ponzi realized he could make even more money if he had investors, and his postage plan rapidly turned into a fiddle. He began using the money from new investors to pay false returns to previous investors. Ponzi attracted thousands of New Englanders by promising sky-high 50% to 100% returns in ninety days, a much more tempting return than the annual 5% they could earn on their savings accounts. At one point, he was said to make $250,000 in a single day. But the scheme finally unraveled when investors tried to claim their money.

By the time of his arrest (for more than eighty counts of mail fraud) on August 12, 1920, Charles Ponzi owed investors nearly $7 million.

A Ponzi scheme is any investment swindle where supposed returns are paid to existing investors with money taken in from new investors. The schemers rope in new investors with the promise of much higher than average returns, ostensibly from blockbuster money-making opportunities with very little downside risk. Early investors receive their promised returns as new money flows in, giving the appearance of real profits from a successful business venture.

But all Ponzi schemes are destined to collapse, as the path to new investors dries up, or as many early investors look to cash out.

INDEX